EQUIP
The Gravity Leadership Playbook

WRITER
Bobby Powers

EDITORS
Brooke Carey, Grant MacLeod,
Jen Peck, James Pratt, and Chloe Vega

VISUAL DESIGNER
Jeremy Salvo

TABLE OF CONTENTS

INTRODUCTION

"Becoming a leader is synonymous with becoming yourself.
It is precisely that simple and it is also that difficult."

-WARREN BENNIS

Making the transition from individual contributor to team lead can be difficult. Some of your close friends may now report to you, and you've probably already been handed a stack of problems to solve that you've never seen before. To compound the difficulty, you may have received a leadership position that other team members also wanted. You aren't sure when you'll ever find the time for your own work in between meetings, answering team member questions, and spearheading team projects.

Take a breath.

It's okay. Every new manager has felt the exact feelings you're experiencing. No one is ever fully "ready" for a management position when they step into it. You were chosen for this role not because you're expected to know everything already, but because you've proven yourself to be a resourceful, creative problem solver. We trust that you can lead the team through periods of calm as well as storms, to figure out the answers to tough problems, and do the right thing when faced with difficult decisions.

This book is meant to guide you through your leadership journey. The transition to management is difficult, and it doesn't happen overnight. Thankfully, there are many other leaders who have helped pave the way, and you can learn from their stories, struggles, and successes. This book is packed with examples from Gravity leaders as well as information from other books, articles, and TED talks that provide a framework for understanding your new role.

Equip is grounded in the idea that to truly create a "Be Your Own CEO" environment, we must not only *empower* people to make decisions, but also *equip* them with the tools they need to be successful.

BYOCEO = Empowering Employees + Equipping Employees

We know you'll face many challenges in this new position, and we want to ease that transition any way we can. Our hope is that this book can equip you in three ways:

1. Distill insights from other leaders into bite-sized content
2. Speed your learning curve for this new role
3. Pose questions to help you consider how you want to handle tough situations you'll face in management

The Importance of Your Role

Managers have a huge influence on employee experience and engagement. In fact, a recent Gallup report showed that managers account for up to 70 percent of the variance in employee engagement.[1] In other words, you can make a large positive impact on your team. You can empower and equip them, push them and challenge them, help them develop and grow.

Your Leadership Style

Every leader has their own personal style, and it's important to realize that everyone leads differently. There is no "right way" to lead. Your leadership style will be based on your values, personality, and past experiences. Over time, you will develop your own personal brand of leadership.

> "There are best practices, but ultimately leadership is about person-to-person relationships. Leadership is challenging because it involves a lot of creativity and discernment around how best to accomplish goals as a team."
>
> **-MATT SAKAUYE (SALES MANAGER)**

One of the biggest mistakes young leaders make is thinking they need to mirror the styles they've seen demonstrated by their previous managers. For instance, maybe you had a

---

[1] Harter, Jim and Adkins, Amy. "Employees Want A Lot More from Their Managers." *Gallup*. 2015.

manager who was firm and direct, or a manager who was warm and friendly. You will be tempted to think that you need to match a specific style, but what matters most is whether your style is true to you.

Here's how a few Gravity leaders define their personal leadership styles:

Phil Akhavan: "I'm friendly and relaxed until something needs to be addressed. Because my natural style is to be friendly, whenever I have to break out of that mold, the team generally takes it seriously."

Edwin Dutton: "I'm fairly tactical as a leader. I'm pretty involved in the details. I think that's helpful for me to understand and improve things, but I hope that I allow people enough freedom and autonomy to do the work and tell me that I'm making mistakes. I hope to create a trusting, collaborative environment that has a strong direction to follow."

Tammi Kroll: "I don't know that I have a single style. I think I've evolved over time. Generally, my style is trying to figure out what makes people tick and what makes them give their all. You have to figure out what that is, then figure out how to feed that passion. I try to find opportunities for people to do what they want to do."

Matt Sakauye: "I like to work from a place of personal connection. Out of connection, you can develop trust, respect, and openness. I want team members to know I care more for them as people than I care about what they do as employees."

Jessica Moore: "In my opinion, there's no one specific leadership style that works for every situation. The leadership theory most aligned with my style is situational leadership. A situational leader adapts their style based on the situation and the team's or individual's needs. When working with my teams, I try to be observant and adapt to react appropriately. In some scenarios, that may look like taking a more hands-on approach and in other situations, you have to give individuals the freedom to fish for answers and make their own decisions."

This Role Is Different Than Your Last One

You've made the shift from individual contributor to manager. Amidst this shift, it's easy to fall into the rut of doing the same work you've done before: grabbing cases out of the team queue, cranking out daily work, answering calls, etc. After all, you're most comfortable with that type of work and you know you're good at it.

The problem with that is you've been put into a *new* role with *new* responsibilities. Your job has changed, so your daily work needs to change with it. You have been tasked with ensuring the team is functioning efficiently and effectively, helping team members enjoy their work, and finding ways to improve our business. Those tasks necessitate that your daily work is different than it was before your role transition.

Here are a few of the responsibilities that come along with your new role: meeting 1-on-1 with team members, helping team members develop career paths and compensation plans, leading team meetings, interviewing and hiring, talking to team members about their performance, letting people go when they're not a good fit for the company, shepherding team projects, representing your team in meetings with other teams, tracking team performance numbers and pushing for greater team efficiency, etc. That's a long list, and there's no way you can continue to do the same work you did before *and* pile on this new list of responsibilities. It just won't work.

It's easy to make one of two mistakes when moving into a management role: staying "in the weeds" or entirely removing yourself from the day-to-day team work. Both extremes are problematic, and you should find the right balance.

If you continue taking a large number of cases, calls, etc., your team will suffer because other team tasks will be dropped. On the flipside, if you stop doing *any* of the daily work, you will become disconnected from the team's responsibilities and may even lose some credibility with the team. Find a balance. Many team leads strike a balance by diving into the team queue occasionally—either on a scheduled basis or when the team's workload becomes temporarily unmanageable. Something similar may work for you.

Impostor Syndrome

You may be wondering, "Do I have what it takes to be a manager?" Leading a team is a big responsibility, so it's perfectly natural to experience some fear and self-doubt.

Sometimes these feelings of doubt can escalate into something called impostor syndrome, which is defined as "a psychological pattern in which an individual doubts their accomplishments and has a persistent internal fear of being exposed as a 'fraud.' Despite external evidence of their competence, those experiencing this phenomenon remain convinced that they are frauds, and do not deserve all they have achieved."[2] We want to tackle this impostor syndrome topic head-on in this Introduction section because these feelings can inhibit self-confidence and impede some of the leadership skills we'll be discussing in this book.

You're not alone if you find yourself thinking things like "I feel like a fake" or "I hope people don't find out I'm actually not that smart." Researchers estimate that almost 70 percent of people experience impostor syndrome at some point in their lives.[3] Many recognizable people have admitted experiencing

[2] Wikipedia contributors. "Impostor Syndrome." *Wikipedia*, 2018. Retrieved Dec 6, 2018.

[3] Sakulku, Jaruwan. "The Impostor Phenomenon." *The Journal of Behavioral Science* 6(1), 75-97. 2011.

impostor syndrome, including Tom Hanks, Sheryl Sandberg, Michelle Obama, and Neil Gaiman. A number of people within Gravity have also encountered it and have gone on record about their struggles so others can understand how common it is: Grant MacLeod, Jen Peck, Bobby Powers, and Jose Garcia. Feel free to reach out to any of them if you ever want to talk about impostor syndrome.

"When I made the transition to management at a prior job, I felt overwhelmed by the number of complex requests I received from my direct reports and my supervisor," says Grant MacLeod (Product Manager). "I wasn't sure what I had said in my interview that made senior managers think I could come up with all the answers. More than once, I desperately needed a pep talk from a mentor, a reaffirmed commitment to trust my own instincts, and to dedicate some time to break down the problems ahead of me into more solvable chunks."

Thankfully, there are several things you can do to mitigate those feelings of doubt. Here are four tips to try:

- **Realize your feelings are normal.** Many people experience this. Chances are good that the list of people above includes one or two people you respect and deem to be successful. If they're struggling with this despite their success, that tells you your self-doubt doesn't come from lack of ability. You are capable, as are they.

- **Stop comparing yourself to others.** Oftentimes feelings of insecurity come from playing the comparison game: "I'm not as good of a leader as _____" or "I don't know anywhere near as much as _____." Thoughts like this are unproductive. Focus on your personal growth and what you want to learn next to become more successful.

- **Keep a record of your successes.** When you're wallowing in self-doubt, it's easy to forget about all the positive feedback you've gotten through the years. It's important to record your successes so you can referring back to them later. For example, you could consider tracking positive comments in a journal or Google Doc, then referring back to those comments when feelings of doubt creep in.

Recognize that failure doesn't make you a fake.[4] You *will* make mistakes. You *will* fail. That's part of life and it's part of leadership. Everyone messes up. Acknowledge your mistakes and move on. "Realize that nobody knows what they're doing," says author and entrepreneur Kyle Eschenroeder. "Nobody knows exactly what is going on. There are a ton of people who will tell you they know the answers. These people are liars. The world we live in is the result of a lot of brave people tinkering, failing, and succeeding once in awhile."

Our hope is that this book inspires deeper conversations about tough leadership questions that can be further hashed out in 1-on-1s, mentorship pair-ups, coaching conversations, manager workshops, and other training sessions. Use this book as your springboard for those conversations.

Each chapter of this book covers a topic that is integral to management. We've hand-selected leaders who do a great job in each area and incorporated their stories, advice, and quotes. Use these leaders as resources. Talk to them if you're struggling with one of these topics. At the end of every chapter, you'll also find a list of additional resources (e.g., books, articles, e-learning trainings) to reference if you want to dive deeper into that topic.

Now, let's get started!

---

[4] Eschenroeder, Kyle. "Overcome Impostor Syndrome: What to Do When You Feel Like a Fraud." *Lifehacker*, 2014.

Additional Resources

Article:
"Complete Guide for New Managers"
by Alison Robins (Officevibe)

Article:
"Overcome Impostor Syndrome: What to Do When You Feel Like a Fraud"
by Kyle Eschenroeder (Lifehacker)

Article:
"6 Leadership Styles: Strengths, Weaknesses, and Examples"
by Swetha Venkataramani (LinkedIn)

Article:
"Overcoming Impostor Syndrome as a First-Time Manager"
by Jackie Berkery (Doist)

Personal Coaching (External):
Utilize our Modern Health benefit program

Personal Coaching (Internal):
Reach out to TA to get paired up with a personal coach

PART 1
KNOWING YOURSELF

CHAPTER 1
VALUES

"It's not hard to make decisions when you know what your values are."

-ROY DISNEY

Before the invention of the compass, sailors and explorers used the North Star to guide them as they navigated the globe. During the Civil War era, runaway slaves also followed the North Star to point the way toward the land of freedom in the northern states and Canada. The North Star serves as a compass to orient people toward where they want to go.

As a leader, your personal values are your North Star. Every day you will face decisions that test your personal integrity. If you haven't clarified your personal values, each decision will require mental exertion and stress. However, if you know what values you want to live by, decision-making will become much easier.

Jen Peck (Director of Engineering) has seen values shape her life in a profound way. "Growing up with a social worker as a mother, equity has sort of driven my life," Jen says. She remembers an incident when she was three or four years old that planted the seed for her personal value of Equity. Jen was with her mom doing a social work home visit and overheard someone insulting a homeless person. Jen couldn't understand why anyone would treat someone so unfairly, and she committed to treating people well—no matter who they were.

"Since that moment, that was my trajectory: I'm going to be kind to people," Jen says. "I feel like we don't define power equally in this society in literally any way, so as much power as we can give people, the better. I think about that from a team perspective, too. I want to be sure that I'm advocating for everybody fairly."

Matt Sakauye says his top values of Family and Teamwork impact his leadership. "Whether you've identified and acknowledged the values or not, they play a big part in how you make decisions and interact with people," Matt says.

Matt's value of Teamwork shows up in the way he structures team goals and activities. He tries to balance competition and collaboration by tracking wins and losses as a team. The group wins *as a team*, and their opponent isn't other employees but other credit card processors.

Values are part "nature" and part "nurture." Your perspective and priorities have been formed by the experiences you've faced in your life. By identifying your values, you can better understand your personal motivations and preferences.

Values Exercise

Through this exercise, you will evaluate and prioritize which values are most important to you.

- Look at the list of values[5] below and cross out words that don't resonate with you.
- Re-read the list and place a checkmark next to the items that are important to you.
- Review the checked items and pick your top five values.

Accountability	Accuracy	Achievement	Adventure
Altruism	Ambition	Assertiveness	Balance
Boldness	Calmness	Carefulness	Challenge
Cheerfulness	Clarity	Commitment	Community
Compassion	Competition	Consistency	Contentment
Control	Cooperation	Creativity	Curiosity
Decisiveness	Dependability	Determination	Diligence
Discipline	Discretion	Diversity	Economy
Effectiveness	Efficiency	Empathy	Enthusiasm
Equity	Excellence	Expertise	Faith
Family	Fitness	Focus	Freedom
Fun	Generosity	Grace	Growth
Happiness	Hard Work	Honesty	Honor
Humility	Independence	Intelligence	Intuition
Joy	Justice	Leadership	Learning
Love	Loyalty	Mastery	Openness
Optimism	Order	Originality	Perfection
Practicality	Preparedness	Professionalism	Quality
Reliability	Results	Security	Self-Control
Selflessness	Self-Reliance	Sensitivity	Serenity
Service	Simplicity	Speed	Spontaneity
Stability	Structure	Support	Teamwork
Thankfulness	Thoughtfulness	Tolerance	Trustworthiness
Truth-Seeking	Understanding	Vision	Vitality

[5] MindTools Content Team. "What Are Your Values?" MindTools blog, 2016. (Abridged content.)

Once you've identified your top five values, write them in the first column of the table below. Everyone has their own interpretation of what each word means, so in the second column, define what each value means to you. Using the third column, rate how well you're currently living up to your definition of each value ("1" means that you struggle with that value and "5" means that you embody that value every day at work and at home).

Your Personal Values

Value	Definition	Self-Eval (1-5)

Identifying your personal values is important because it will help you make better, faster decisions that are in concert with what's most important to you. If you pay attention in the coming weeks, you'll notice your values show up in the way you live your life and lead your team.

Fundamentally, leadership is all about knowing yourself. The better you know yourself, the better you can lead others.

> "Identifying values doesn't mean you're going to be perfect—you're kind of creating your own leadership constitution, defining the things that are most important to you. At the end of your career, you want to be able to say, 'I governed myself according to these things.'"
> **-RON PRICE AND STACY ENNIS**

Tammi Kroll (COO/CTO) says her top values are Ownership, Curiosity, Tenaciousness, and Helping Others Succeed. Those values inspired her to offer a dev boot camp for employees. "Shortly after I came to Gravity, I got the impression that people were looking for more career opportunities," says Tammi. "In talking with lots of people, we had several who were interested in enhancing their careers with software development. Knowing that Gravity's next growth step was adding some technology to the portfolio, I saw the need for developers. From that was born the idea of seeing how many people might want to learn how to develop software.

"We decided to put together a hack day where people would have two weeks to develop something, anything, starting from whatever point they were at. The winner of the hack day would be sent to a development boot camp. The competition ended with a tie, so we sent two people to boot camp!" Tammi says. Tammi's goal was to find people who had a passion and curiosity to learn new things and help them succeed.

Differences in Values
Each person's values are slightly different, and these differences can occasionally create conflict. For example, a manager who values Carefulness may find it difficult to work with someone who values Spontaneity. Conflict like this is natural, but you must ensure that these differences don't cause you to become biased against those whose values differ from yours.

Tammi says she has to consciously remind herself that her values may not align with another person's values. "Because there are certain things that I really value, if people don't exhibit those same values, there might be times when I don't value that person as much as I should," she says. "Maybe they have ten other traits that make them great, but if they're lacking some of these things, I may not fully appreciate the value that person brings to the table until I get to know them better. It's important for all of us to remind ourselves that everyone's values and styles are different. I'm not going to force my values on someone else if they've had success doing it their way."

Start with WHY

Great leaders understand how their personal values drive their behavior. Great leaders also seek to determine their sense of personal purpose—what we refer to as your "WHY."

Author Simon Sinek says, "It's not about what we do, it's about why we do it."

> "Very few people or companies can clearly articulate WHY they do WHAT they do. When I say WHY, I don't mean to make money—that's a result. By WHY I mean what is your purpose, cause, or belief? WHY does your company exist? WHY do you get out of bed every morning? And WHY should anyone care?"
>
> -SIMON SINEK

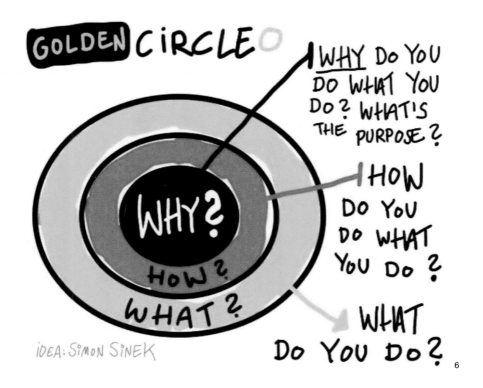

GOLDEN CIRCLE

WHY DO YOU DO WHAT YOU DO? WHAT'S THE PURPOSE?

HOW DO YOU DO WHAT YOU DO?

WHAT DO YOU DO? [6]

WHY?

HOW?

WHAT?

IDEA: SIMON SINEK

Strong WHYs attract others who have like-minded interests. From a business perspective, a strong WHY can sometimes attract more prospects than a low price or a fancy new feature.

You're already familiar with our company's WHY: "We stand with the little guy or gal who believes in the American dream and is willing to work to chase it." That mission drives everything we do at the company. It also sets us apart. Many small businesses can sense the WHY behind what we do by how we interact with them, and they want to be part of what we're doing.

Many companies market and sell their product or service based on their WHAT rather than their WHY. For our company, selling based upon our WHAT would sound something like this:

[6] Angelus, Richard. "Start With Why: The Golden Circle (Chapter 3 Summary)." Idea for Today blog, 2018.

"We can help you process credit card transactions so you can make money for your business. Want to work with us?"

Leading with WHY rather than WHAT sounds much different: "We're passionate about helping small businesses. We want to be a true partner to you and help you understand what you're paying so you can better compete with the Goliaths in the industry. Want to work together?" Doesn't that sound far more compelling? The WHY distinguishes a generic sales pitch from an inspiring invitation to join a movement.

Similarly, from an individual perspective, leaders who are driven by a strong WHY often inspire more followers than more experienced or more intelligent leaders who aren't guided by a strong WHY.

Finding Your WHY

Now it's time for the big question: what drives you personally?

The answers to the questions below can serve as subtle indicators for your personal WHY statement.

What makes you excited to get up every morning?

_____

_____

_____

_____

What types of tasks make you feel most energized at work?

_____

_____

_____

_____

What has been your proudest accomplishment?

_____

_____

_____

_____

Who do you really enjoy helping?

_____

_____

_____

_____

What does success look like to you in your life?

_____

_____

_____

_____

What does success look like for you in this role?

_____

_____

_____

_____

What themes do you notice in your answers above?

_____

_____

_____

_____

Using what you've learned about yourself from these questions along with the "Personal Values" section earlier in this chapter, try to develop an elevator pitch for your WHY. Rather than focusing on the value you provided as an individual contributor, focus your thoughts on the value you want to provide as a leader and mentor to others. Your WHY should guide the way you grow and improve your team and the company.

Start with this outline:

My WHY is to _____

_____ so that _____

_____."

Write down as many ideas as you want until you find one that clicks. Dig deep. It should not be something superficial. Continue to pull back the layers until you find a statement that resonates with you on a deep, emotional level.

_____

_____

_____

Here are a few examples of WHY statements from Gravity leaders:

- *Rosita Barlow:* "Every individual deserves an opportunity to understand the depths of their natural talents and how those talents align with that person's passions, values, and career. I want to give every individual that opportunity regardless of whether I manage them."

- *Matt Sakauye:* "To make a difference in whatever place I'm in and whatever person's life I have the opportunity to impact."

21

- *James Pratt*: "To live harmonious change."

Because his personal WHY statement is about making a difference in people's lives, Matt Sakauye's relationships with his team stretch outside work. "In many instances, with the people I work with, I've gotten to walk alongside them through positive as well as difficult life events, like having kids, getting divorced, dealing with medical issues, etc.," he says. "Those kinds of things are going to impact people's performance a fair amount, so I want to be there to offer support, guidance, and empathy."

Understanding your WHY is an ongoing process. Your passions and motivations may change over time, and that's okay. The best thing you can do is continuously explore your own motivations and become comfortable with the difficult self-reflection that is necessary to answer questions like the ones posed above.

Values Tips

Make time for self-reflection. Unfortunately, it's easy to get caught up in the busyness of our day-to-day lives and not take time to self-reflect. Plan time for meditation, journaling, walks, or other opportunities to self-reflect.

Be patient with yourself. It can take a lot of introspection to discern what is most important to you and what deeper purpose drives you.

Respect differences. Each person has a different perspective and background that influence the way they prioritize things in their life and work. Be mindful of those differences and respect each person's values.

Additional Resources

Book:
Start with Why
by Simon Sinek

Book:
Principles
by Ray Dalio

Book:
Growing Influence
by Ron Price and Stacy Ennis

E-Learning:
LDU talk on "Be Your Own CEO"
by Jen Peck

TED Talk:
"How Great Leaders Inspire Action"
by Simon Sinek

CHAPTER 2
STRENGTHS AND WEAKNESSES

"The job of a leader is to build a complementary team, where every strength is made effective and each weakness is made irrelevant."

-STEPHEN R. COVEY

Often, our personal values offer subtle hints about our strengths and weaknesses. For instance, someone who values perfection will often generate high-quality work but may sacrifice speed and efficiency in order to reach their desired outcome. Someone who values optimism will likely exert a positive presence on the team but may struggle with providing accurate timelines because they are overly optimistic about how quickly they can complete their work.

Thinking back to the chapter about values, what could your values indicate about your leadership tendencies?

_____

_____

_____

_____

Personal Strengths and Weaknesses

Every leader has strengths and weaknesses. It's important to learn as much as you can about both in your quest to become a stronger leader. Knowledge of your strengths will help you determine where you can best move the needle for your team and the company. Knowledge of your weaknesses points toward areas where you'll need others' help in order to succeed.

The best leaders find ways to utilize their strengths as much as possible while surrounding themselves with people who can do things they cannot do. By focusing on your strengths and letting others do the same, you and your team members will be more productive, engaged, and fulfilled.

What do you see as your top 3 personal strengths?

1) _____

2) _____

3) _____

On the flipside, what do you see as your top 3 weaknesses?

1) _____

2) _____

3) _____

Think back to a recent project. What went well or poorly with that project and how might that reflect on your strengths and weaknesses? Does that information agree or disagree with what you listed above?

_____

_____

_____

_____

_____

_____

_____

3x3x3 Exercise

We like to believe that we know ourselves well, but sometimes others can see things we cannot see.

To form a more complete picture of your strengths and weaknesses, take a few minutes to ask three people about what they see as your top three strengths and your top three weaknesses. As a form of 360-degree feedback, try to ask your boss, one direct report, and one close friend to each provide honest, direct answers to this question. Record their thoughts below.

Feedback from Direct Report

TOP STRENGTHS	TOP WEAKNESSES
1)	1)
2)	2)
3)	3)

Feedback from Boss

TOP STRENGTHS	TOP WEAKNESSES
1)	1)
2)	2)
3)	3)

Feedback from Close Friend

TOP STRENGTHS	TOP WEAKNESSES
1)	1)
2)	2)
3)	3)

What patterns did you observe in their feedback? How does their feedback compare to your personal assessment?

_____

_____

_____

_____

_____

_____

_____

Strengths and Weaknesses Tips

Build a complementary team. Determine the strengths and weaknesses of each team member. Whenever possible, allow people to work within their area of strength and hire people who will balance out your team's existing strengths. A diverse team is much stronger and more creative than a homogeneous team.

Share your weaknesses. The more comfortable you are talking about your struggles, the more comfortable your team members will be as well. In the words of philosopher Jean Vanier, "I am struck by how sharing our weakness and difficulties is more nourishing to others than sharing our qualities and successes."

 Seek an outside perspective. We will never have an unbiased perspective about ourselves, our accomplishments, and our struggles. That's why it's important to constantly seek out feedback from others. Look for ways to seek outside input about your leadership to ensure you're not relying too much on your own perspective.

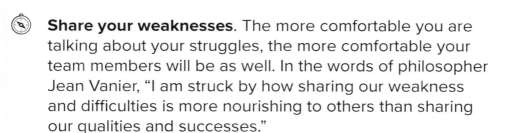

Additional Resources

Article:
"Best Tests to Help You Understand Your Strengths and Weaknesses"
by The Forbes Coaches Council

Assessment:
VIA Institute on Character provides a free character strengths assessment that some employees have found useful

Book:
StrengthsFinder 2.0
by Tom Rath

Book:
Strengths Based Leadership
by Tom Rath and Barry Conchie

CHAPTER 3
VISION AND GOALS

"If you want to build a ship, don't drum up people to collect wood and don't assign them tasks and work, but rather teach them to long for the endless immensity of the sea."

-ANTOINE DE SAINT-EXUPÉRY

Vision

In this chapter, we're not going to talk about how to build a vision statement. There are countless books and articles written on that topic, and many result in businesses creating pithy one-liners that don't actually change behavior. Instead, we're going to briefly discuss what it means to develop true vision as a leader and how to enact that vision by setting goals with your team.

At its core, vision means knowing where you want to go and why you want to go there. It is *not* telling people what to do, but rather developing a shared understanding of what is truly important and working together to create a better future.

Take a few minutes to respond to these questions to start considering your vision.

What do you hope to accomplish with your team?

_____

_____

_____

_____

Why is that important to you? What would look different within the team, company, or customer relationships if you achieved that?

_____

_____

_____

_____

Don't stress if you don't have a vision in mind right now. It will come with time. As you work with your team, you'll begin to unearth the ultimate impact you want the team to have upon our company, employees, merchant experience, etc.

Goals

Whereas your vision describes where you want to go, your goals explain how you plan to get there. Goals narrow our focus. They help us prioritize and tell us what is truly important.

> "A few extremely well-chosen objectives impart a clear message about what we say 'yes' to and what we say 'no' to."
> -ANDY GROVE

Goals allow us to break a big concept (like a vision or a 5-10 year plan) into manageable chunks. These manageable chunks help us envision the path to success. They also prevent us from wallowing in despair by thinking about how large and unattainable a 5-10 year plan seems when we look at it in isolation.

Multiple studies have shown that productivity skyrockets when employees have well-defined goals that challenge their current abilities.[7] Goals improve accountability, ownership, and engagement. Even the act itself of setting goals encourages self-reflection and creativity.

How We Set Goals

It's often tempting to write generic, ambiguous goals like "Improve customer service" or "Shorten turnaround time on case requests," but such goals are not helpful because they are not specific. A well-written goal explicitly conveys what we're aiming to accomplish. At the end of the month/quarter/year, we should be able to look back and unambiguously determine whether we accomplished what we set out to do.

One of the best ways to write effective goals is to use the "SMART goals" technique. Although SMART goals have become ubiquitous, the concept is worth reviewing because it is a powerful idea that can make us more effective.

There are numerous definitions of the "SMART" acronym, but we'll follow this one:

- **Specific** - Well-written goals define what "done" looks like. They are specific enough that anyone should be able to objectively state whether the task was accomplished.

---

[7] Doerr, John. *Measure What Matters: How Google, Bono, and the Gates Foundation Rock the World with OKRs*. Portfolio, 2018.

- **Measurable** - Whenever possible, goals should be quantitative or measurable. Rather than "Improve customer service," a better goal would be to "Increase our net promoter score (NPS) from 30 to 40 by December 2019."

- **Attainable** - Every goal we set should be realistic. Unrealistic goals can be demotivating, which is the opposite of what we're trying to achieve. It's good to stretch current abilities, but we don't want to take that too far.

- **Relevant** - Every goal should be something worth doing. An irrelevant goal is one that would have little to no impact on the team or business, even if we accomplish the goal.

- **Time-Bound** - Set deadlines. Put a date on every goal. For instance, notice how the NPS goal above references that the improvement should happen *by December 2019*. Without that date, it would be difficult to gauge success.

Goal-Setting Tips

Put goals in writing. Writing your goals makes them tangible. It takes them out of the ether of *ideas* and into the substance of *action*.

Make your goals visible. Tape them to your desk, computer monitor, or wall. Visibility keeps everyone focused on the goal. While serving as TA team lead, Emery Wager started every weekly team meeting by reviewing the team's "BHAG" (big, hairy, audacious goal). After reviewing the BHAG, every team member shared what they planned to do that week to progress toward the overarching goal.

Incorporate accountability. Share your goals with others so they will keep you accountable to achieving them. For team goals, assign portions of the goal to individual team members. Kimberley Paterson (Finance Team Lead) divided her team's five primary functions into separate objectives that could be owned by individual team members. Kimberley said that strategy enabled each team member to have ownership and accountability over the team's work.

Whenever possible, connect team goals to company goals. Doing so ensures your team stays focused on the biggest things our company has identified to be successful. It also shows team members their work is significant and meaningful.

Balance input and output goals. Input goals articulate what *actions* you're going to perform, whereas output goals articulate what *outcomes* you hope will come from those actions. In other words, input goals are controllable, while output goals are often dependent upon outside forces. For example, an Outside Sales Rep may set an input goal of knocking on 50 doors per day and an output goal of bringing in $5,000 in new revenue each month. By setting both types of goals, we can better delineate what is fully within our scope of control while also working toward big initiatives that may depend upon external factors, like a merchant agreeing to process with us.

Break big goals down into smaller ones. Too often, we set goals that are so broad that it's hard to determine what we can do today to begin working toward the goal. How can you take action *today*? Set mini goals for every day, week, or month. James Pratt (VP of People Development) writes daily and weekly goals onto 3x5 cards, then carries those cards with him wherever he goes. Each week, he retrospects on how many of his weekly goals he accomplished and how he may need to work differently the following week to be more productive.

- ⏱ **Build in checkpoints to stay on track.** If you have a goal to finish something by the end of the year, determine how much progress you want to make by the end of the first month, quarter, etc. Use those checkpoints as timelines to evaluate your progress.

- ⏱ **Retrospect.** If you're one month into a one-year goal and you're far behind where you expected to be, step back and think about what could be wrong. Brainstorm new ideas for completing the goal.

- ⏱ **Edit your goals as necessary.** If your original goal turns out to be unmanageable or irrelevant as you gather more information, edit the goal. Goals are meant to drive action and accountability—two things that will be in short supply if you determine the goal wasn't appropriate in the first place.

- ⏱ **Know WHY you're pursuing each goal.** When things get difficult, understanding the deeper meaning behind the goal can help you push through.

Additional Resources

Book:
Measure What Matters
by John Doerr

Book:
Built to Last
by Jim Collins and Jerry Porras

Book:
Scaling Up
by Verne Harnish

CHAPTER 4
LEADING YOURSELF

"Nothing so conclusively proves a man's ability to lead others, as what he does from day to day to lead himself."
-THOMAS J. WATSON

When talking about leadership, it's natural to immediately begin talking about how to lead *others*. However, it's important to recognize that one of the core aspects of leadership is leading yourself.

Specifically, when we say the phrase "leading yourself," we're referring to two things:
1. Becoming a person worth following
2. Completing your own work

Becoming a Person Worth Following
The fact that you're in this role demonstrates that the company values you as a person of integrity. You've proven yourself to

be trustworthy and capable. But the work is not over. Your job is to continue improving and developing your leadership ability.

One of the best ways to do this is to keep learning. Ask team members to teach you about their areas of expertise. If you as the manager are willing to humble yourself and learn from everyone else, it will set the expectation that others on the team should do the same.

When he started in his new role, Phil Akhavan (Inside Sales Manager) consumed books about leadership and personal development, then shared those insights with the team. Others began to follow his example by reading and sharing insights of their own.

> "Leadership and learning are indispensable to each other."
> -JOHN F. KENNEDY

Seek out a mentor who can teach you more about how to grow and develop a team. When looking for a mentor, don't limit yourself to only people within our company. There are thousands of capable leaders out there who would be honored to meet over lunch or coffee to share their insights.

LinkedIn is a great place to find potential mentors. Search your LinkedIn network to find individuals with experience in the areas you want to learn. For instance, maybe you just moved into a Sales Manager role and you want to learn from other Sales Managers at tech companies who have been in their role for two years or more. Plug those characteristics into a LinkedIn search and see who turns up.

Broaden your search beyond your "1st tier connections" (the people you personally know) to also search your "2nd tier connections" (people who are connected to one of your connections). It's likely that one of your connections—possibly even someone at Gravity—knows a person who would be a great potential mentor for you.

Completing Your Own Work

One of the most common difficulties for new managers is finding time to complete their "own work." Amidst a sea of meetings, 1-on-1s, team projects, and team member questions, you probably feel like there is little time to complete anything *you* want to do.

Whenever you feel frustrated about not completing your own projects, remember that *your team is your job.* This is a fundamentally different role than the individual contributor role you had before. Your new position isn't about you; it's about them. The purpose of your job is to find opportunities to help them speed up, even if that slows you down.

Urgent vs. Important

It's easy to run from one fire to another, constantly jumping from urgent task to urgent task. In this way, we tend to prioritize reactive, urgent work over proactive, important work.

> "What is important is seldom urgent and what is urgent is seldom important."
> **-DWIGHT EISENHOWER**

The important things that will truly move the needle for us, our team, our company, and our customers often don't scream loudly for our attention. Hence, we don't prioritize them, and we get pulled into other work instead.

U.S. President Dwight Eisenhower developed a personal system for gauging urgency versus importance. Below is a version of Eisenhower's matrix with a few modern examples listed in each quadrant.

	URGENT	NOT URGENT
IMPORTANT	**Quadrant 1** Important calls/emails Appointments Emergencies Projects with deadlines	**Quadrant 2** Career growth Relationships Preventative tasks Maintenance Exercise
NOT IMPORTANT	**Quadrant 3** Some calls/emails Some meetings Shallow relationships Some phone alerts	**Quadrant 4** Social media TV/Movies Gossip Trivial tasks

Eisenhower often plotted his work into this type of matrix, which helped him prioritize what to do first.

Tasks in Quadrant 1 tend to get handled because they are both important *and* urgent. For example, if a merchant calls or emails to say they cannot process transactions right now, that would definitely qualify as a Quadrant 1 task which should be handled before doing anything else.

Most of us need to consciously set aside time to focus on Quadrant 2 tasks because although they are very important, they don't scream loudly for our attention. Common Quadrant 2 tasks include resolving engineering "technical debt," creating training materials, and cleaning up inaccurate data in Salesforce. It's often helpful to schedule time to complete Quadrant 2 tasks to ensure we don't neglect them.

---

[8] Swope, Stephenie."Understanding the Eisenhower Matrix." Epiphenie blog, 2016. (Modified image.)

Quadrant 3 tasks are urgent (or at least appear to be urgent), but they don't truly move the needle to make us or our clients better. One common example of a Quadrant 3 task is getting invited to a call or meeting even though you're not the best person to make a decision on the topic at hand. Quadrant 3 tasks can often be delegated to someone else who is in a better position to handle the situation.

Quadrant 4 tasks are neither urgent nor important, yet they distract us from more meaningful work. The best modern-day example is social media. Social media companies design their software to *seem* important and urgent (e.g., flashing red dots for new messages and notifications), but tasks like checking social media are neither urgent or important. The more we can resist Quadrant 4 work, the more productive we can be.

If we're able to prioritize important work (tasks in Quadrants 1 and 2), we'll become more effective with the things that matter most.

Leading Yourself Tips

Block time in your calendar for important projects. If you need to accomplish something, schedule it. Block out the necessary time, then protect that time.

Don't take other people's monkeys.[9] In your new role, a lot of team members will come to you with problems. Some of those problems will be yours to solve while others will be best solved by the team member. If someone is trying to take a "monkey off their back" and give it to you, don't let them. Whenever possible, guide someone to how they can proactively solve the problem themselves. By doing so, they will become more capable

[9] Blanchard, Ken, William Oncken Jr., and Hal Burrows. *The One Minute Manager Meets the Monkey*. William Morrow and Company, 1989.

and you will free up more time for other work.

Allocate time for "deep work." Recognize the difference between urgent work and important work. Sometimes the best way to complete important projects is to disconnect from Slack, email, phone, etc. for a period of time. Deeper work generally requires blocks of uninterrupted time. Emery Wager (Business Development) and Rosita Barlow (Director of Sales) frequently "hide" in phone booths and conference rooms in order to focus on deeper projects. You may need to do the same. Just find the appropriate balance, as you also want to ensure you're around to help the team whenever possible.

Know when to say "no" to additional projects. Everyone has limited bandwidth. Evaluate any new project against your WHY, your vision, and your personal/team/company goals. If there's not alignment between those things and this new project, reconsider whether you're the right person to do it or whether it should be done at all.

Additional Resources

Article:
"Managers, Stop Collecting Monkeys!"
by Bobby Powers (Medium)

Book:
Deep Work
by Cal Newport

Book:
The One Minute Manager Meets the Monkey
by Ken Blanchard, William Oncken Jr.,
and Hal Burrows

Book:
The Effective Executive
by Peter Drucker

Book:
The 7 Habits of Highly Effective People
by Stephen Covey

LinkedIn:
Search your network for possible mentors

PART 2
SERVING YOUR TEAM

CHAPTER 5
MANAGING FORMER PEERS

"Where weak leaders demand trust be given to them, servant leaders inspire it."
-SIMON SINEK

We often promote people from within to lead their current team. If you recently made that transition, you understand that managing former peers can be challenging. Some of your closest friends may be on the team, which can make performance conversations even harder than they already are.

Thankfully, others within Gravity have made similar transitions and can provide advice on how to handle your new management role while maintaining close personal friendships. One of the best ways to strike that balance is by setting ground rules for your team interactions.

Personal Ground Rules

Every leader must come up with their own ground rules for interacting with team members. Should you grab beers after work with the team? If your best friend is on the team, how can you keep that relationship strong without showing favoritism?

Every leader's answer to these types of questions will be slightly different (and subjective). Above all, seek to be fair and recognize that your actions have consequences. Like it or not, people will be watching how you conduct yourself. Be mindful of that and consider how your actions could be perceived by the team.

Here are a few things to ask yourself about your interactions:

- **Happy hours** - It's common for teams to get together after work to grab drinks and socialize. When those situations arise, do you want to join? If you do, how many drinks will be your max?

- **Social media** - Are you going to be Facebook or Instagram friends with your team members? If you decide to connect with team members online, what will you do if/when you see one of your team members post something controversial (e.g., complaining about the company, making sexist or offensive comments)?

- **Sharing information** - As the saying goes, "Knowledge is power." If you only share information about upcoming company changes with certain team members (e.g., those whom you know well outside of work), other team members may view that as favoritism. How are you going to ensure you communicate in a way that doesn't create a knowledge imbalance on your team?

Phil Akhavan discovered the benefit of setting personal ground rules when he stepped into his first management role.

"When I started in my role as a new manager, I didn't have any personal ground rules for what I should or should not share with the team," says Phil. "Because of that, I probably said more than I should have in some conversations while in other conversations I came off as too guarded and unwilling to share. Now that I've been in the role for a while, I've decided on some ground rules for myself. One of those is that I won't talk to other team members about someone else's performance. I still maintain close personal relationships with team members, but I try to not share more details with members of the team that I have developed a closer relationship with."

Talk to other managers to hear how they've managed the transition to leading a team for the first time. Try things for yourself, then decide what works best for you.

Others Who Wanted Your Role

If you just stepped into a management role, it's likely that someone else on the team wanted that role as badly as you did. Your job is now to work with that person to uplift them, support them, and help them develop a career path for their growth and development.

The best way to move forward is to have an honest, vulnerable 1-on-1 with that individual within the first week of starting in your new role. Acknowledge that you're aware they applied for the role, reaffirm their value to the team, and relay that you're in their corner and will do anything you can to help them succeed. You can also look for an opportunity to let them lead an upcoming project or company-wide initiative.

James Pratt has found it helpful to explicitly ask for help from people who wanted the role. For example, you can ask someone, "Would you be willing to be an advisor and help me identify blind spots?" Questions like this exhibit disarming humility, which helps that person know you're on the same team to help each other become successful.

How Can You Get People to Follow You?

It's easy to get stuck on this question, but it's generally the wrong question to ask. Worrying about making others follow you directs your focus inward (on you) when your focus should instead be outward (on them). A better question to ask is "How can you help your team members do *their* jobs and attain *their* goals?" The more you focus on helping others, the more they will *want* to follow you.

Rosita Barlow uses John Maxwell's book *The 5 Levels of Leadership* to frame her thoughts on leadership. Maxwell describes the five levels of leadership as follows:

Level 1: Position — People follow because they have to

Level 1 leaders have influence solely due to the position they hold. This is the starting point for most new managers. They are afforded respect due to their position but haven't yet reached a point of true leadership and influence.

Level 2: Permission — People follow because they want to

Leaders at this level have built relationships of trust within their team. Team members follow the leader out of desire rather than mere compliance. This is the first step of true leadership.

Level 3: Production — People follow because of what you have done for the organization

At this level, the leader has begun to generate results. They are achieving the expected business metrics, and others can see the way the leader has positively impacted the company.

Level 4: People Development — People follow because of what you have done for them personally

Leaders at this level empower others and invest time in developing other leaders. They put others first and think of ways to develop others who can go on to lead their own teams.

Level 5: Pinnacle — People follow because of who you are and what you represent

Pinnacle leaders (those with a strong WHY) do not compromise their personal ethics in order to generate short-term results. Leaders who lead with integrity leave a legacy for others.

In other words, people will naturally follow you as you help them, generate results, and stand up for your beliefs. Leaders often move through these levels in a linear fashion, and many never reach Level 5 leadership. Leadership is a journey—not a destination—and we're all at a different point in that journey. While Level 5 leadership is a worthwhile aspiration for everyone, it is difficult to reach because it often requires a lifetime of hard work.

Based on Maxwell's 5 levels of leadership, which level do you think you're at right now? Why?

_____

_____

_____

What are the things you need to work on to reach the next "level"?

_____

_____

_____

What's something you can do this week to help one of your team members achieve their goals?

_____

_____

_____

Managing Former Peers Tips

- **Set ground rules in advance.** Think through what types of difficult situations you may experience as a new manager. Decide in advance how you'd like to handle those situations if they arise.

- **Ask other managers for their advice.** Schedule 1-on-1 time with two or three other Gravity managers. Ask them what lessons they've learned from their time in leadership.

- **Be fair to everyone.** Fairness means that you will treat everyone justly and not show favoritism. Counterintuitively, fairness does *not* mean you will treat everyone the same. In fact, part of leadership is recognizing that each person is unique and may require something different from you. "Each person is wired differently and has a different background than everyone else," Matt Sakauye says. "The way that you handle a certain situation with each person is going to differ. The more that you can understand your communication style and also the communication style and motivators of each person you're working with, the more likely you are to be able to adapt to a situation in the way that's going to be most helpful."

Additional Resources

Article:
"How to Manage Your Former Peers"
by Amy Gallo (*Harvard Business Review*)

Article:
"What to Do First When Managing Former Peers"
by Liane Davey (*Harvard Business Review*)

Book:
The 5 Levels of Leadership
by John Maxwell

E-Learning:
LDU session on "Managing a Team"
by Rosita Barlow

CHAPTER 6
DECISION MAKING

"If your employees believe their job is to do what you tell them, you're sunk."

-SUSAN SCOTT

Most companies make decisions in a top-down manner. The CEO makes decisions that will be enacted by the VPs, who make decisions that will be enacted by the Directors, and so on down "the chain of command."

We think that decision-making model is outdated and ineffective. Whenever possible, we want the individuals closest to a decision to make the decision. Whoever has the best context should be the one who takes action. Oftentimes, that will be someone on the front lines who is dealing directly with our merchants. For instance, if one of our Support or Deployment Reps has more context on a decision than their boss or their boss's boss, the Support or Deployment Rep should be the default decision-maker. At other times, the team lead or another person in management may have more context. In those instances, that manager should decide. Regardless, the decision should be pushed to those who have the most and best information.

We would miss out on a lot of great ideas if we based every decision on what the CEO, COO, or team lead thought about the situation. Those in management roles are supposed to help facilitate decisions and discussions, not make all of the decisions themselves.

Confident Humility

Being a manager does not mean you are expected to know everything or make all of the decisions. Far from it. The best leaders listen first and talk second. You will gain more respect by gathering insights from your team than you will from dominating conversations with your own ideas.

A good rule of thumb is to exhibit "confident humility." Be confident in what you know, and ask for help with what you don't know. Look to others when they're the expert and confidently contribute when you're the expert.

Making Decisions with Incomplete Information

"Oftentimes in a leadership role, you get about 30 percent of the information you need to make a decision," says Jen Peck. "Sometimes you make a bad decision and you have to be okay with that. You have to be less risk-averse because you have to be willing to fail and to make those bad decisions knowing that it's going to go successfully sometimes and not so successfully other times. And you learn from it. You learn over time."

Because we often won't have all of the necessary information to make a decision, we must choose when to pull the trigger on a decision. Some leaders prefer speed and some prefer accuracy. There often is not a right answer, which is why it's important to gather insights from others whenever possible to help you see multiple sides of the problem.

"The key to life in a lot of ways is balance," says Edwin Dutton (Director of Finance). "You need to be balanced in your approach between speed versus certainty, but weight your approach based on the consequence. Taking risks and failing is really okay. I think in order to learn or to get better at making decisions, you have to fail often. That goes for people who go too quickly and too slowly. You have to understand that taking the risk is okay."

You will make mistakes and so will others. When you find out that a decision didn't turn out as you expected, take time to reflect on what happened. Make the effort to understand whether you could have done something better.

Decision-Making Tips

Make more decisions at the front lines. Whenever possible, it's best to have those closest to the client make decisions that will impact clients.

Keep others in the loop. Consider who else needs to know about the decision you or your team is making. Should you involve more people in the decision? How can you generate buy-in across all of the relevant groups? Should you loop in your manager to get their perspective?

Balance speed and quality. We want to move fast but we also want to make the best decision possible with the information available. Work to strike an appropriate balance between speed and quality.

Additional Resources

Book:
Thinking in Bets
by Annie Duke

Book:
Black Box Thinking
by Matthew Syed

Book:
Creativity, Inc.
by Ed Catmull with Amy Wallace

Book:
Farsighted
by Steven Johnson

CHAPTER 7
DELEGATION

"Never tell people how to do things. Tell them what to do and they will surprise you with their ingenuity."

-GENERAL GEORGE PATTON

Now that you've moved into a management role, it will be crucial for you to develop the skill of delegation. Delegation is not merely a tactic of minimizing your personal workload; it is one of the foremost ways to develop your people and give them stretch assignments to grow and improve.

Most Gravity managers have expressed a tendency to err on the side of delegating *too little* rather than *too much*. You can often tell if you're not delegating enough by evaluating what type of work you're completing and how much you have on your plate. For example, if you keep canceling meetings or postponing important projects, that's a sign you're taking on too much responsibility. If you find yourself doing 50 percent of your old job (e.g., helping with cases or administrative work) on any given day rather than a more appropriate number like 10-20 percent, you may need to delegate more of those tasks to your team.

There are a number of reasons why you might struggle with delegation:

- **You think you can do something better yourself.** Maybe you can, but at what cost? Are you the only person who can perform that task or are you simply the best person to do it? If someone else can do that task 80 percent as well as you can, maybe that is enough.

- **You don't trust anyone else to do it.** This could be a red flag that you haven't developed capability within your team. Your job is to develop your people, so if there is truly no one else capable of doing this task, you should work to develop your team's competency in that area and ensure you're not siloing knowledge.

- **It's easier to do it yourself.** Yes, that's undoubtedly true. But how often does this task arise? If the task needs to be done every week, month, etc., then teaching someone else how to do it and delegating it to that person will likely save time and make life easier in the long run.

- **You worry that your employees are too busy.** Everyone is busy, including you. Sometimes the only way for you to avoid long hours and burnout is to spread the love by delegating more work to others on the team. If you're concerned they may have too much going on, you can always check with them regarding their capacity and use that information to determine how much to delegate at that time.

- **You aren't sure what to delegate.** There's no formula for what to delegate, so try asking yourself a few questions to determine whether delegation is the right decision in a particular situation: Is this task or decision something I'm uniquely able to handle? Is this task a core element of my job? Could a team member grow by taking on this opportunity?

Remember that the primary purpose of delegation is not to get rid of your own work but to develop your team and find opportunities for them to grow. While delegation is not always the right answer, it is a useful skill to develop in order to distribute work, develop others, break down silos of knowledge, and free yourself up for other strategic initiatives within the team and the company. Effective delegation is a long-term investment.

The 7 Levels of Delegation

In addition to delegating specific tasks, you might also choose to delegate decisions. When you delegate a decision, you're trusting someone else to make that decision on your behalf, or, at the very least, giving them an opportunity to suggest a solution you can discuss together.

Each business situation is slightly different. Some decisions are best made by you, while other decisions are best made by one of your team members, another leader, or someone else within the organization. You may even decide to delegate certain aspects of a project but not others. For example, a Customer Support Team Lead may decide to delegate a project to collect customer service data but may want to be one of the key decision-makers for determining what action steps the team should take based upon the data collected.

The following model, developed by entrepreneur Jurgen Appelo,[10] provides a helpful framework to understand the various levels to which you can delegate decisions:

1. **Tell** - You make the decision yourself. You may decide to explain your rationale to others.

2. **Sell** - You decide which decision you think is best, then try to sell others on your idea.

3. **Consult** - You ask for input before deciding and try to consider other people's opinions in your decision.

4. **Agree** - You discuss the decision with everyone and seek group consensus on the decision.

5. **Advise** - You allow others to decide, but you offer an opinion for them to consider.

6. **Inquire** - You let others decide but ask them to sell you on their decision afterward.

7. **Delegate** - You leave the decision entirely up to someone else and tell them they don't need to follow-up with you.

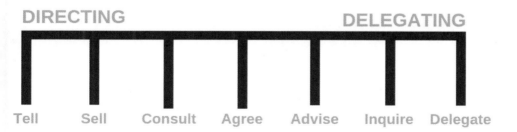

[10] Appelo, Jurgen. "The 7 Levels of Delegation." Medium, 2015.

Things to Consider When Choosing a Delegation Level

- **How quickly do you need to move on this decision?** When speed is of the essence, you'll likely want to choose one of the "Directing" levels on the left-hand side of the graph. Too much discussion could slow the process down to the point where any action is no longer effective. For example, it may be best to choose "Telling" or "Selling" in situations where a merchant cannot process, a partner needs something completed in the next couple of hours, or we're in violation of a compliance policy that needs to be rectified quickly. On the other hand, if you're trying to improve a department process, you might entrust someone on your team with the responsibility of figuring out what needs to be done and executing on whatever plan they determine is best. Whenever possible, allow others to have a stake in the decision-making process.

- **How important is this decision and how many people will it impact?** The greater the importance and impact of a decision, the more certain you want to be. You'll likely want to choose an option toward the middle of the graph that incorporates many people's ideas.

- **Can one or two other people on your team learn something from making this decision?** By picking an option on the right-hand side of the graph, you can give others a growth opportunity by letting them make the decision.

Think about one decision you are currently facing. Which model do you think would be best for that decision? Why?

_____

_____

_____

Regardless of how a decision is made, you want to fully own the decision and be accountable for it. That means that if you have delegated the decision to someone else, you will not throw them under the bus if their decision doesn't work out. You are jointly responsible for the decision.

Delegation is a skill that can simultaneously expand your capacity and develop your team's capability. Become an effective delegator and you'll be impressed by the results.

Delegation Tips

Identify the right person. Pick someone who can learn from the activity, yet still has the skills to accomplish the task. Try to pick someone who has enough bandwidth to tackle the project or decision. Dan Price (Founder and CEO) says, "If the person's plate is only 60 percent full, I'm more likely to delegate to them. But if they're closer to 95 percent of their capacity, I might just do the task myself to not stress them out."

Define the *what* and the *why*, but delegate the *how*. Share the relevant background information so the team member knows why the task is important. No one wants to work on meaningless tasks or things they don't understand. Explain *what* has to be accomplished and *why* it's important, but let the team member decide *how* to do it.

Define what "done" looks like. Talk to the team member and decide upon a shared definition of what success looks like for this project. For example, when the person is done with the work, do they just need to close a Salesforce case? Follow-up with you to let you know it's finished? Circle back with a merchant or Sales Rep? Ensure you and the team member agree on what exactly must be done.

Clarify who is owning what. Using the "7 Levels of Delegation" model above, discuss with the team member what level of involvement you should have in the project. Should the employee run their idea past you before they act? Who is making the ultimate decision? Setting expectations up front ensures that everyone is on the same page for what exactly you are delegating.

Find the balance. If you delegate something and continue to stay heavily involved, the team member may feel like you don't trust them. On the flipside, if you completely disconnect and never check in with the team member, they may view you as disengaged or unwilling to help. The key is to clarify your expected level of involvement early on. Ask the team member what you can do to support them and how they'd like you to be involved.

Agree on a timeline. When should this project be completed? Is there an external date from a merchant, partner, vendor, or employee that you need to hit?

Determine project milestones. If the project is large and complex, it may be helpful to determine a few key milestones. Milestones help chunk the work into smaller tasks, but they can also give you a few agreed-upon touchpoints when you can check in with the team member without feeling like a micromanager.

Additional Resources

Article:
"The 7 Levels of Delegation"
by Jurgen Appelo (Medium)

Article:
"23 Tips on How to Delegate Work Effectively"
by Duncan Muguku (ThriveYard)

Article:
"7 Strategies for Delegating Better and Getting
More Done"
by Jayson DeMers (Inc.)

E-Learning:
LDU talk on "Delegation"
by Lisa Edwards

E-Learning:
LDU talk on "Situational Leadership"
by Lisa Edwards

CHAPTER 8
RECEIVING FEEDBACK

"Leaders who don't listen will eventually be surrounded by people who have nothing to say."

-ANDY STANLEY

Receiving critical feedback is one of the most difficult things about working with others. When we know we're about to receive feedback, our blood starts pumping faster, and we immediately begin to feel defensive. But in a company like ours that values direct communication and constant feedback, you will inevitably struggle as a manager if you can't find a way to learn from feedback.

"I think receiving feedback is a learned behavior," says Ian Nisbet (HR Manager). "When you're getting feedback, your initial reaction is to try to fight back or prove wrong whatever people are trying to tell you. For me, it's taken a while to not only get over that in my head but to turn that around into a craving for feedback. If you listen to feedback and you take it in, it's definitely going to have an effect on how you do things down the road."

Feedback Blockers
Unfortunately, there are many factors that block us from accepting and acting upon feedback. Some are biological, while others are psychological. Understanding more about these blockers can help us overcome them.

Feedback Blocker #1: Hormones
Two hormones cause problems for us in our struggle to accept and act upon feedback: cortisol and adrenaline.

Cortisol is the stress hormone. It heightens our awareness of threats and increases our heart rate to prime us for handling the threat. From an evolutionary perspective, cortisol was useful to help us perceive threats from predators. Although we no longer have to deal with those types of predators in our daily lives, cortisol still drops into our system whenever we perceive a threat. Unfortunately, this means that our bodies produce cortisol when we believe we're about to receive feedback. Our bodies experience feedback as a threat to our peace of mind and wellbeing.

Once feedback has been shared with us, the "threat" is confirmed and our bodies produce adrenaline. Adrenaline focuses all of our body's energy and resources upon the threat at hand, and blood is diverted into our muscles (and away from our brains). Rational thinking goes out the window. Adrenaline triggers our "fight or flight" reaction, which is why many people respond to feedback by either becoming defensive or trying to end the conversation.

In other words, our bodies are working against us in our efforts to receive feedback. While we cannot stop our bodies from producing these two hormones, we can gradually train ourselves to view feedback as a positive rather than a negative. Training ourselves to not see feedback as a threat can lower our stress levels and help us truly hear what others are saying.

Feedback Blocker #2: Mental Stories

Our brains are hardwired to process the world through stories. We often make observations, then filter those observations through the lens of what would make sense in a story. These narratives are often judgmental or counterproductive, and three archetypes show up time and again: villain, victim, and helpless stories.

Villain Stories

It's easy to write a villain into the story. The villain could be an upset merchant who is using colorful language to voice their frustration. It could also be a team member who disagrees with us about a choice we think the team should make. In the case of feedback, the "villain" is often the person giving the tough message.

Victim Stories

If someone else is the villain, we're generally the victim. We assume the other person is intentionally trying to be hurtful, and that we are the innocent ones taking the fall for something that is not our fault.

Helpless Stories

Helpless stories don't necessarily have a villain or a victim. Instead, we craft a mental story about how we are entirely helpless in a situation (e.g., we have no time to do something, we cannot change our personality traits).

Think about a recent time you received feedback from someone. From the three story archetypes above, which mental story did you tell yourself?

_____

_____

_____

_____

What are the drawbacks of telling yourself that story? What is another story that would fit those same facts?

_____

_____

_____

_____

What negative stories do you hear your team members telling about other teams or our merchants? How will you respond the next time you hear a story like that?

_____

_____

_____

_____

Feedback Blocker #3: The 3 P's

Because it's uncomfortable to hear critical feedback, our brains unconsciously search for reasons to invalidate the feedback we receive. Three "P's" block us from truly listening to the feedback others share with us: the Person sharing the message, Personal feelings, and the Packaging of how the person gave the message.

Person

Our brains are critical of who is sharing a message with us. We may discount a message that's coming from a direct report—especially one whom we think is inexperienced, young, old, or [insert your own judgmental adjective here]. Yet, we may make an immediate behavioral change when the same message comes from a boss or peer.

We form snap judgments of people, and unfortunately, those snap judgments linger in our heads longer than they should. These impressions are often inaccurate or incomplete, but they influence the way we process messages from that person.

> "If we're serious about growth and improvement, we have no choice but to get good at learning from just about anyone."
> -DOUGLAS STONE AND SHEILA HEEN

We need to remember that everyone offers a unique perspective that can shed light on how we are being perceived by others. We shouldn't let our biases about someone get in the way of receiving a message we need to hear. We should be agnostic about the messenger.

Personal

Personal feelings often block us from hearing tough messages. This occurs due to a psychological concept called cognitive dissonance.

Cognitive dissonance is defined as "the mental discomfort (psychological stress) experienced by a person who simultaneously holds two or more contradictory beliefs, ideas, or values. This discomfort is triggered by a situation in which a person's belief clashes with new evidence perceived by that person. When confronted with facts that contradict personal beliefs, ideals, and values, people will find a way to resolve the contradiction in order to reduce their discomfort."[11]

This dissonance frequently manifests when we receive feedback. We think of ourselves as good people: we work hard, we're trying our best, and we have positive intentions. However, sometimes we receive feedback that runs counter to those personal beliefs. If someone gives us feedback that we aren't working fast enough, that conflicts with our personal belief that we are doing a good job. Rather than wrestling with the dissonance, our brains rush to one of two conclusions:

1. We stick with our original feeling that we are a great employee, and we discard the feedback.
2. We discard our original feeling that we're doing a good job and think that we must be a bad employee based on the feedback we received.

Both extremes are bad. Cognitive dissonance encourages us to accept one extreme or the other: we're a good employee *or* we're a bad employee. We need to embrace the dissonance and walk into the gray area: we are a good employee who simply made a mistake. This opinion is much more nuanced and accurate than accepting either extreme. Accepting the nuanced opinion enables us to embrace feedback and use it to improve.

Another mistake we tend to make when receiving feedback is to jump to a conclusion regarding what that feedback means about us as individuals. We assume the feedback speaks to our *identity*, when in fact it refers only to a specific *action or inaction* of ours that could have been handled better.

---

[11] Wikipedia Contributors. "Cognitive dissonance." Wikipedia, 2018. Retrieved Dec 26, 2018.

Here are a few examples of what this looks like:

What the speaker says:	What we hear:
"You haven't completed as much as I expected you would this week."	"I'm a terrible employee, and I'm going to lose my job."
"When you said _____ in the meeting, I felt disrespected. You could have been more kind in sharing your opinion."	"I am a complete jerk."
"I've been feeling distant from you lately. It seems like you keep pushing me away."	"I am a lousy partner/spouse/friend, and this relationship is not going to work."

We often make snap judgments about how we should feel about ourselves based on just a few sentences. The problem is that as soon as we begin to question our identity, our emotional barricades go up. We miss out on the message and fail to learn the lesson we're supposed to learn from that situation.

The key is to recognize that feedback almost always refers to a specific behavior rather than our personal identity. Once we make that important mental shift, we begin to truly hear what others are saying.

Another personal impediment to accepting feedback is our ego. Pride blocks our ability to process and fix mistakes. Counterintuitively, the best people in any given field often recognize they have the most to learn. High performers often see feedback as valuable data to be marshaled into personal improvement and new behavior.

> "As our island of knowledge grows, so does the shore of our ignorance."
> -JOHN ARCHIBALD WHEELER

Packaging

Unfortunately, most of our learning will come from people who don't give feedback well. It would be easy to discount every message that is "packaged" poorly, but doing so would lead to stagnation rather than growth. We cannot control the way others give us feedback, but we can absolutely control the way we respond to that feedback.

Maybe the person giving the feedback was shouting, crying, swearing, or misinformed. But what did they say? Was there a nugget of truth buried deep in the message?

Even if 90 percent of the message is off-base, almost every message contains a golden 10 percent we need to hear. As soon as we orient our minds to search for these nuggets of truth, our personal development skyrockets.

Learning from feedback demands that we make a life decision to be continuous learners who prioritize the truth over fuzzy feelings and sugar-coated messages. Personal growth requires the ability to learn from everyone in every situation.

To recap, three forces block us from accepting feedback:
1. Two hormones: cortisol and adrenaline
2. Mental stories: villain, victim, and helpless
3. The 3 P's: person, personal, packaging

Feedback Tips

- **Develop a habit of asking for feedback.** Ryan Pirkle (Marketing Director) has built enough trust with his team that he refuses to let his team members leave their 1-on-1 meetings with him until they've shared feedback about how he can improve. Feedback becomes easier to receive the more you ask for it.

- **Mentally prepare to receive feedback.** As a leader, you will receive a lot of feedback. It can sometimes be overwhelming to receive so much feedback. If you are about to go into a 1-on-1 or another meeting in which you expect to receive difficult feedback, you can mentally prepare by taking a few long, deep breaths; going on a short walk to clear your mind; or reminding yourself that feedback is one of the best ways to grow as a leader.

- **Listen deeply.** Give the other person time to share their thoughts. Don't interrupt or cut them off. Listen from the perspective that the person is just trying to improve you and/or the situation for the future.

- **Don't think about your response while the other person is talking.** Ian Nisbet recommends, "Turn off the part of your brain that is always trying to react to what people are saying." If you can do that, you'll be able to listen rather than immediately formulating a defensive response.

- **Say "thank you."** Before you respond with anything else, thank the person who gave you the feedback. Recognize that it takes a lot of courage to share feedback.

- **Don't be defensive.** Try to view feedback constructively rather than personally by viewing it as an opportunity to grow and develop.

Uncover their path. Ask questions to understand the other person's perspective and see what you're missing. Find out how they reached their conclusion.

Find the nugget of truth. Even if you disagree with some of the message and the way the person shared it, there's always something you can learn from what they said.

Follow up. Circle back with the other person later after you've had the chance to put their feedback into practice. Ask them whether they've noticed an improvement and ask them for accountability.

 # Additional Resources

Book:
Thanks for the Feedback
by Douglas Stone and Sheila Heen

Book:
Principles
by Ray Dalio

E-Learning:
LDU talk on "Receiving Feedback"
by Bobby Powers and James Pratt

CHAPTER 9
GIVING FEEDBACK

"One of the most important insights anyone in business can have is that it's not cruel to tell people the truth respectfully and honestly."

-PATTY MCCORD

Direct communication is one of the things that makes our culture unique. One of the best ways we can protect and improve our company's culture is to lead by example by sharing direct feedback.

Employee engagement firm Officevibe found that 65 percent of employees want more feedback.[12] They also found that 82 percent of employees appreciate receiving feedback, regardless of whether it's positive or negative. Giving feedback to your team members is one of the best ways to help them

---

[12] Robins, Alison. "Employee Feedback: The Complete Guide." Officevibe, 2019.

improve and accomplish their goals.

What Happens When Feedback Isn't Shared?
Bobby Powers (Head of Learning & Development) discovered the tough answer to this question when he was 24. As a freshly minted MBA grad, he accepted a management position leading a team of 50 people in a retail store. A couple of months into that role, he had to fire one of his team leads—a person who had been with the company for five years.

The termination discussion went about as poorly as one could imagine. Security guards ultimately had to escort the employee out of the building as he yelled and swore at his now-former co-workers.

Although it was difficult to go through this situation as a new manager, Bobby says this experience taught him two things:

(1) Refusing to share feedback is unkind and unfair.
Bobby found out that every one of this employee's past managers had been too scared to share feedback. The employee had a long history of treating customers and co-workers poorly, but despite numerous complaints, no one had addressed the issue with him because they feared he would respond aggressively. No one told the employee there was a problem, so he kept behaving the way he always did.

(2) Softening tough messages doesn't help anyone.
"When I first began working with this employee, I shared critical feedback cautiously and infrequently," Bobby says. "I sandwiched feedback between compliments and didn't clearly tell him how his behavior was impacting the rest of the team. If I had done a better job of sharing direct, candid feedback, this employee would have realized the significance of the problem and perhaps would have changed his behavior. At best, he may have kept his job. At worst, he at least wouldn't have been as surprised when the day came for us to let him go."

Unfortunately, this sort of thing happens all the time. A team member has a performance issue. Managers and peers notice, but no one has the guts to address the problem. Everyone hopes the problem will go away on its own, but instead it escalates until, eventually, the person's employment is called into question. A manager finally talks to the team member about the problem, but by that point, everyone is so frustrated that the team member is destined for failure. The team member cannot improve quickly enough and either loses their job or, at least, the respect of their co-workers. We want to avoid those situations at all costs.

We Have a Misguided Sense of Kindness

These problems occur because we have a misguided sense of kindness and value our personal comfort over others' growth. We are hardwired to believe that criticism is unkind because it could potentially hurt someone else's feelings. But which is more unkind: being honest with people so they have the opportunity to improve or setting them up to fail because they don't realize there is a problem with their performance?

> "Over the past several years, my team and I have learned something about clarity and the importance of hard conversations that has changed everything from the way we talk to each other to the way we negotiate with external partners. It's simple but transformative: Clear is kind. Unclear is unkind."
> -BRENÉ BROWN

Unfortunately, when your greatest fear is causing emotional pain to someone, you cause even greater pain to your team. You lower the quality standard on your team, permit problems to fester, and allow people to get fired when they might have been able to improve.

Giving feedback is not easy, but it's one of the most selfless things we can do. We need to value others' growth over our personal comfort.

Feedback Tips

⊙ **Share feedback early and often.** Don't wait to give feedback to someone else. It's important to share your message while the situation is still fresh in your mind and theirs. If it's not possible to give immediate feedback because you're running off to a meeting or that person is talking to someone else, leave yourself a reminder to follow-up with them as soon as possible.

⊙ **Assume positive intent.** We have no way to know the causes of others' actions. By assuming positive intent, we make it easier to have a conversation without things getting heated. Ask yourself, "Why would a reasonable, rational, and decent person do what this person is doing?"[13]

⊙ **Acknowledge the difference between intentions and actions.** "We judge ourselves by our intentions and others by their behavior," says author Stephen M.R. Covey. By distinguishing between intentions and actions, we can better understand how to critique a person's behavior without critiquing the person.

⊙ **Start with questions.** Because you don't know the other person's intentions, it's best to start with questions rather than statements. We know what we've observed, but we don't know anything about the other person's story. Questions are the key to unlock their story and hear their perspective.

⊙ **Use the situation/behavior/impact model.** Share the specific situation and the behavior you observed. Then talk about the impact that person's behavior had upon

[13] Patterson, Kerry, et al. *Crucial Conversations: Tools for Talking When Stakes Are High*. McGraw-Hill Education, 2011.

the team, clients, etc. Talking about impact is important because it helps the other person connect their actions to the consequences of those actions.

Be as specific as possible. Regardless of whether you're sharing positive or critical feedback, provide specific details. Rather than complimenting someone by saying, "You're a great public speaker," instead express what the person did that made you think that about them: "In that training, you provided relevant stories that connected well with the audience. You didn't stammer or refer back to your notes, which made it clear you knew the content well. I think you did a great job with that presentation." Providing details helps people know explicitly what they should continue doing or stop doing.

Facts are better than interpretations. Facts are the least controversial and most persuasive way to express candor. Sharing facts (e.g., "You've closed twenty cases this week") rather than interpretations (e.g., "You are working slowly") opens the door to further discussion. When we begin with objective information, we encourage the other person to share objective information as well.

Make eye contact. Making eye contact communicates to the other person that you are engaged in the conversation, that they have your full attention, and that you are confident in the message you are giving. Avoiding eye contact can come across as dehumanizing, unconfident, or impersonal.

Don't sugarcoat or "sandwich" feedback. Under the guise of kindness, we often try to soften feedback. Unfortunately, the more justification we provide and the more we downplay a difficult message, the less likely the person is to receive the message we're trying to share. When sharing tough messages, we must be direct and assertive. That's not to say that we can never share positive messages along with critical ones, but in doing so, we must be abundantly clear with our critical feedback to ensure the core message is not lost.

 # Additional Resources

Book:
Crucial Conversations
by Kerry Patterson, Joseph Grenny,
Ron McMillan, and Al Switzler

Book:
Difficult Conversations
by Douglas Stone, Bruce Patton, and Sheila Heen

Book:
Fierce Conversations
by Susan Scott

Book:
Radical Candor
by Kim Scott

E-Learning:
LDU talk on "Giving Feedback"
by Bobby Powers

CHAPTER 10
LEADING MEETINGS

"While it is true that much of the time we currently spend in meetings is largely wasted, the solution is not to stop having meetings, but rather to make them better. Because when properly utilized, meetings are actually time savers."

-PATRICK LENCIONI

When she became team lead of the Finance team, Kimberley Paterson decided one of her first actions would be to reimagine the team's meeting structure.

Many of the Finance team members felt the team's current weekly meetings were ineffective. While no one fell asleep during the meetings (usually), the meetings were often lackluster or unproductive. "Our meetings would go one of two ways," Kimberley says. "Either it would be a really heated topic where everyone had opinions on it and we just didn't have enough time or data to actually dive into it, or we would come in with nothing to talk about and we would just small-talk or chat for an hour. Either way, it wasn't really effective."

Looking for inspiration, Kimberley turned to Patrick Lencioni's book *Death by Meeting*. While reading the book, Kimberley realized her team had been making a number of classic meeting mistakes.

Common Meeting Mistakes

- There is no clear purpose, expectations, or agenda for the meeting.

- The meeting starts and/or finishes late, which wastes time and impacts everyone's schedules for the rest of the day.

- A few team members dominate the discussion, meaning that the group's opinion sways toward the opinion of the "vocal minority" while the opinion of the "silent majority" goes unstated.

- Team members introduce tangents that either distract from the primary discussion or are not pertinent to all attendees.

- The group tries to discuss too many topics in a single meeting, including mixing tactical and strategic topics.

- Nobody from the team conducts research before the meeting or brings data to the meeting, which means the team cannot make informed decisions during the meeting.

- People don't understand what's at stake in the meeting and why the decision is important, so they lose focus and disengage.

- The meeting concludes without assigning action items, owners, and timelines for next steps.

- Attendees don't share their opinions or voice their disagreement, resulting in groupthink.

> "When a group of intelligent people come together to talk about issues that matter, it is both natural and productive for disagreement to occur. Resolving those issues is what makes a meeting productive, engaging, even fun."
> **-PATRICK LENCIONI**

Having now identified some of their meeting mistakes, Kimberley decided to share her observations with the team. In the next Finance meeting, she described what problems she had noticed in their meetings and asked others to share their thoughts. Every team member agreed that the meetings needed to change.

Kimberley proposed that the team adopt an idea from *Death by Meeting*: hosting three different kinds of team meetings.

1. **Daily standup (<15 minutes)**
   - Focus: Quick updates from each team member about daily priorities and roadblocks
   - Examples: Specific cases in the queue, other meetings in the day, who needs help, etc.

2. **Weekly tactical meeting (45-90 minutes)**
   - Focus: Tactical issues regarding what the team needs to accomplish in the week, along with a quick "lightning round" of who is working on what
   - Examples: Key team projects, upcoming OOO time and coverage plans, updates, etc.

3. **Monthly strategic meeting (2-4 hours)**
   - Focus: Decide how to handle one or two specific, complex issues within the team or company
   - Examples: Proposed changes to team processes or structure, how to handle a recurring complex issue or client concern, etc.

After a few weeks of trying the new meeting structure, Kimberley circled back with the team to find out what they thought of the changes. Every single team member agreed that the new meetings were more productive than the old ones.

The meeting format above may or may not work for you; every team is different. The key is to find the right structure and frequency that works best for your group. It's also important to be flexible to ensure your team meetings continue to meet the needs of the team. Kimberley and the team have decided to frequently revisit their meeting format to keep their meetings efficient and relevant. You'll likely want to do the same.

A good meeting can actually save a lot of time. Focus on making every meeting productive by using the tips below and asking team members for their feedback and ideas on how to improve team meetings.

Meeting Tips

- **Decide if a meeting is necessary.** Don't host a meeting if an email or Slack update will work instead. For example, many project updates can be shared more efficiently via email than in a meeting.

- **Clarify the purpose of the meeting.** At the start of each meeting, briefly remind attendees what you're trying to decide in the meeting and explain what is at stake from the decision.

- **Prepare in advance.** Bring all of the necessary data to make decisions in the meeting.

- **Invite all of the relevant decision-makers.** If some of the decision-makers are not present, you'll end up reaching a half-conclusion, then scheduling a second meeting to convince the other people who didn't attend the first meeting. Avoid double-work by including everyone who needs to be in attendance right off the bat.

- **Only invite *necessary* attendees.** Fewer people is better. The more people you have in a meeting, the less productive it will be.

- **Encourage productive disagreement.** Conflict is good because it gets all knowledge out into the open. Don't allow disagreement to go unspoken because unspoken disagreement often leads to issues down the road.

- **Conclude every meeting by discussing action items.** Decide *who* will do *what* by *when*. Assigning action items ensures that something tangible will come out of your discussion.

- **Iterate upon your meetings.** Adapt the length and format of your team meetings as you determine what works and what doesn't work.

 # Additional Resources

Article:
"How to Lead Effective Team Meetings"
by Dan McCarthy (The Balance Careers blog)

Book:
Death by Meeting
by Patrick Lencioni

E-Learning:
LDU talk on "Leading Meetings"
by Kimberley Paterson

PART 3
DEVELOPING
YOUR TEAM

CHAPTER 11
COACHING

"Tell less and ask more. Your advice is not as good as you think it is."

-MICHAEL BUNGAY STANIER

Although we may not say it in these words, many of us believe that the more we know, the more we'll be able to give advice to other people. After all, it's rewarding to help others, and if we're able to give advice that resonates with someone, we feel happy and fulfilled.

However, when you really think about it, sharing advice is predicated on the belief that we know something another person does not. Although that may very well be the case, people often respond best when they're given the latitude to make their own decisions. If someone is able to reach an insight on their own, they often feel more engaged, bought-in, and excited for what they need to do to solve a problem.

Loosely stated, there are three different response strategies when someone comes to you with a problem:

1. **Advice** - Bring your expertise to bear in order to solve the problem. Use your knowledge and pattern recognition (i.e., what you've seen work in similar situations) to suggest potential solutions to the problem.

2. **Ask Leading Questions** - Formulate an idea of what the other person should do in their situation. Rather than explicitly telling them what you think, ask questions to lead them to a conclusion so it feels like their own idea. This is sometimes called "the illusion of empowerment."

3. **Coaching** - Set aside your experience and simply ask questions. Be curious. Ask open-ended questions to help the other person determine their *own* solution—one that works for them in this specific situation.

In this chapter, we're going to focus on the coaching model because it aligns closely with our "Be Your Own CEO" mindset. Whereas giving advice imparts our personal biases and ideas upon another's situation, coaching helps the other person come to their own realizations. Basically, coaching is *helping others solve their own problems*. It is a framework that promotes self-sufficiency and gives others the tools to think about the problems they're facing in a new way.

Coaching is not the right answer for every situation. Some situations are better suited for giving advice instead, such as when a team member has exhausted many of their own ideas and is interested in hearing how you solved a similar problem. However, learning how to become more "coach-like" is a valuable skill that will help you develop into a more empathetic, people-first leader.

Whole, Resourceful, Capable, and Creative

Thinking like a coach means approaching problems from the perspective that every single person is whole, resourceful, capable, and creative. In using a coaching mindset, we do not assume that we have all the answers. We do not assume that the other person needs to be fixed. We instead assume that they possess the skills and the insight to figure out the answer to their problem and do what they need to do.

The Benefits of Coaching

James Pratt is certified as a coach through the International Coach Federation, a worldwide nonprofit organization dedicated to professional coaching. He's been applying coaching skills for years—both professionally and personally.

"Coaching is by far the most effective way I've found to solve problems. Coaching goes beneath the surface of the problem to find out what the real problem is," James says. "It is a sustainable way of helping people solve their own problems."

James credits coaching for helping him realize how much he truly cares about other people and the personal stories that made them who they are today. As a coach, your job is to truly understand where the other person is coming from and ask open-ended questions to help the person explore their situation from a new perspective. James says this requires the coach to stay in the mindset of "They've got this. They just may not know it right now."

Thinking about conversations from a coaching mindset can be difficult. It requires you to relinquish control over the conversation and instead trust the other person's ability to solve their own challenges. Doing so can be uncomfortable, especially at first. But the outcomes reached via coaching conversations are generally stronger and more sustainable than those reached by giving advice or asking leading questions. Why? Because the other person has fully bought into the solution. The solution has been tailor-made to fit their needs because they came up with it.

Coaching is a great way to support your team members, learn what challenges they're facing, give them an environment to develop their own path, make their own decisions, and take ownership of their development. Just like many of the skills in this book, coaching is difficult to master, but you can see immediate benefits from making small changes.

Coaching Tips

Ask open-ended questions. Open-ended questions (those that cannot be answered with a mere "yes" or "no") provide the other person with the opportunity to reflect and share their thoughts. While closed-ended questions force the other person to choose between options you have created, open-ended questions open up many possible paths for the discussion.

Utilize questions that start with "What" or "How." Whereas questions that start with "Why" tend to make presumptions or suggest solutions (e.g., "Why did you...", "Why wouldn't you just..."), questions that start with "What" or "How" tend to give the other person full latitude to share their ideas. Here are a few examples:
- "What's on your mind?"
- "What's the real challenge here for you?"
- "What outcome are you hoping for in this situation?"
- "How can I help?"

Remain inquisitive. If you approach the conversation with curiosity rather than thinking about the problem as your responsibility to solve, you will be able to do a better job of asking questions rather than giving advice.

Ask one question at a time. We all have a natural desire to ask strings of questions. Asking multiple questions at one time can create confusion or anxiety for the other person in the conversation, so it's best to instead ask one question at a time. Once that question has been answered, ask your next question.

Don't offer advice with a question mark attached. We've all asked questions like "What do you think about [this idea]?" or "How would it work if you [did it like this]?" Such questions are simply advice masquerading as coaching questions. When coaching someone else, stick with honest, genuine questions and resist giving advice in the form of a question.

Become comfortable with silence. Silence is often a signal that you've asked the right question. Allow the other person to think in quiet. Do not fill the space with more questions.

Resist the urge to tell people what to do. Author and coaching expert Michael Bungay Stanier[14] says that coaching is "a little more asking questions and a little less telling people what to do." Stanier says that as a coach, you'll frequently be asked for advice and you can still give it, but first respond with something like, "That's a great question. I've got some ideas, which I'll share with you. But before I do, what are your first thoughts?"

Strategically utilize closed-ended questions. Although open-ended questions are foundational to coaching, closed-ended questions can be used to encourage commitment at critical junctures in the conversation, such as the following examples:

---

[14] Stanier, Michael Bungay. *The Coaching Habit: Say Less, Ask More & Change the Way You Lead Forever.* Box of Crayons Press, 2016.

- "What I heard you say was X, Y, and Z. Does that resonate?"
- "You said you wanted to achieve X, Y, and Z in this conversation. Have we achieved those goals?"

 Recognize that coaching is not always the answer. Sometimes an employee truly needs your guidance, and it's better for you to share advice rather than asking coaching questions. However, even in those situations, utilizing some of your coaching skills and asking "What" and "How" questions can help you learn more about the problem at hand before immediately sharing your thoughts.

 # Additional Resources

Article:
"Core Compentencies for Coaching"
by the International Coach Federation

Book:
The Coaching Habit
by Michael Bungay Stanier

Local Organization:
inviteCHANGE Coaching Organization
(We've used them in the past for coaching workshops)

Personal Coaching (External):
Utilize our Modern Health benefit program

Personal Coaching (Internal):
Reach out to TA to get paired up with a personal coach

CHAPTER 12
1-ON-1s

"One-on-ones are one of the most important productivity tools you have as a manager."

-ELIZABETH GRACE SAUNDERS

You've been on the receiving end of 1-on-1s for awhile. Stepping in as a new manager, the temptation will be to simply run those meetings the same way *your* boss ran them, which may or may not be an effective way to do it.

The Importance of 1-on-1s

Meeting personally with every member of your team is extremely important. These meetings are often your best opportunity to develop a deeper relationship of trust and honesty with each team member while talking about topics that don't arise in everyday discussions (e.g., personal goals, career path, job satisfaction).

There are three primary purposes of 1-on-1s:

1. Build a relationship between you and the team member
2. Find out how you can support the team member
3. Help the team member grow

Prioritize this individual time with your team members, and try to avoid canceling 1-on-1s at the last minute. Frequently canceling 1-on-1s sends a message that those meetings aren't important to you. Work with each team member to decide the ideal frequency you'd like to meet together. Generally, meeting together once every 1-2 weeks is ideal, typically for 30-60 minutes.

Opt for more time together (more frequent meetings or longer meetings) if you and/or the team member are new in your respective roles or if you don't get to see the team member often because they work remotely. You'll need more time to build rapport and trust with each other. Scale back your meetings as necessary once you get going. Typically, more senior team members will need less 1-on-1 time, so adjust accordingly as you get to know your team and what they need from you.

Who Should Run the Meeting?
Many people say that it's most effective for the direct report to run the 1-on-1 to ensure they're getting what they need from you. Having the team member lead the meeting also puts the onus on them for their personal development, which is a good idea.

However, as with so many things in leadership, there's no "right way" to do 1-on-1s. Whatever you decide, we encourage you to be explicit with each team member about which of you will be setting the agenda and running the meeting. Regardless, block out time to prepare for the meeting. As you're just starting to have 1-on-1s, you may want to set aside 15 minutes to prepare for each meeting, which should primarily be focused on the questions you want to cover in the meeting.

Come with questions, but yield more time to the team member if they have things they need to discuss. Let them do most of the talking while you play a supportive role in the conversation by listening and asking thoughtful questions.

If desired, you can always provide more structure or even introduce a few standard topics for every 1-on-1. Kim Scott, the author of *Radical Candor*, asks her direct reports to structure 1-on-1s around four questions[15]:

1. What's on your mind this week?
2. How happy were you this past week?
3. How productive were you this past week?
4. What feedback do you have for me?

Better Questions Yield Better Answers
What questions have you asked in 1-on-1s that did not yield great answers?

_____

_____

_____

_____

If you ask generic questions in your 1-on-1s, you're going to get generic answers. For instance, if you are worried your team member may be getting burnt out from working long hours, don't ask, "How are things going?" That question will undoubtedly yield a blasé response like "Good" and nothing more.

[15] Laraway, Russ. "How to Have Effective 1:1s." Radical Candor blog, 2019.

Be more direct and selective with the questions you ask. If you're curious about burnout, ask questions like "How many hours did you work last week?" By leading with sincere, direct questions, the team member will know that you expect a direct response about that particular issue. After hearing their response, follow-up by asking how you can help and whether you can take anything off their plate. Team members want to know you're aware of their struggles and willing to help.

What is a better, more direct way of asking the questions you listed above?

_____

_____

_____

_____

Vulnerability

Be vulnerable and encourage vulnerability. Leading with vulnerability means leaning into uncertainty and emotional exposure. Vulnerability is saying "I don't know" rather than faking it. Vulnerability is sharing tough feedback you've been given and asking for accountability to improve.

If you're having trouble connecting with a team member, talk about a problem you're facing right now and ask for their help. Vulnerability encourages vulnerability. Open up to them and they'll be more likely to open up to you.

> "Vulnerability doesn't come after trust—it precedes it. Leaping into the unknown, when done alongside others, causes the solid ground of trust to materialize beneath our feet."
> -DANIEL COYLE

Topics for 1-on-1s

As much as possible, avoid using your 1-on-1s to get and give status updates. While a few day-to-day topics will always arise in 1-on-1s, the primary focus of these discussions should be strategic issues and questions that don't surface every day.

Keep an eye out for these warning signs that may signal your 1-on-1s have become too focused on status updates:

- Your team member makes comments like, "Can we cancel today's 1-on-1? I have no updates to share with you today."

- Your 1-on-1s feel boring and stale.

- You don't know your team member's career goals.

- You can't remember the last time you and the team member talked about something they want to learn or do.

To help guide your questions during 1-on-1s, consider using the following "Gravity 4-Square."

1) PERSONAL	2) TEAM
• Hobbies/interests • Family • Personal successes and struggles	• Progress toward goals • Team projects • Relationships with coworkers
3) FEEDBACK	4) DEVELOPMENT
• For you • For them • For the team • For the company	• Career goals • Job satisfaction • What they want to learn • Next role/project

This tool can help ensure that you're learning about each aspect of your team member's life and work. It's important for you to understand these facets of your team members, but there's no formula for what this should look like in any given 1-on-1. Some managers talk about a little of everything in every meeting, while others only talk about strategic questions like career development on a monthly or quarterly basis.

As a starting point, you'll find a list of potential questions below that will help you dig into each area of the 4-Square.

1) Personal Questions
- What are your favorite hobbies outside of work?
- I haven't met your family before. Can you tell me more about them?
- What was your biggest struggle this week?
- Of everything you've done recently, which one thing are you most proud of?
- What is the most important thing you and I should be talking about?
- As your manager, I am going to worry about what matters to you. What are the things that worry you?
- What part of your responsibilities are you avoiding right now because you don't have the time or resources to do it?
- What do you wish you had more time to do?

2) Team Questions
- Who do you admire on the team and why?
- Who on the team deserves more recognition for a job well done?
- What things are you doing that you would like to stop doing or delegate to someone else?
- What conversations are you avoiding right now?
- What would you say are our team's three biggest priorities right now?

3) Feedback Questions
- What is the biggest feedback you have for yourself?
- What strength aren't you using right now?
- If you were me, what would keep you up at night?
- What do you think is my greatest weakness as a leader?
- What can I do to be a better manager for you?
- What's the most de-motivating thing I've done to you in the past few months?
- What do you think is the biggest flaw in our culture?

- What do you think our team/company should be focused on this next month/quarter/year?

4) Development Questions
- What are the things you're most passionate about? Is there a way for us to structure your work more around those passions?
- What are the things you most want to learn in the next three months?
- What strength are you working to develop right now?
- What do you envision as your next role or responsibilities?
- What projects would you like to take on in the coming months to push yourself?

What questions above do you want to begin asking in your 1-on-1s?

_____

_____

_____

_____

Tim Finlon (Sales Trainer) says that before he came to Gravity, his managers at other companies always led 1-on-1s in their own way without seeking out Tim's opinion for what he needed in the 1-on-1. Tim contrasts that with the way his current manager, Rosita Barlow, leads their meetings. Rosita doesn't micromanage the relationship or enforce a certain 1-on-1 framework upon Tim. She lets him lead the meetings, which helps him feel greater ownership of the discussion and his work. By letting Tim guide the agenda, Rosita is also able to see whether their priorities are aligned: *Are we thinking about the same things? Do we have a shared focus for the department?*

Tim says that Rosita also helps him improve by asking challenging strategic questions like, "Is what you're working on now going to help us three years or five years down the road?" Their 1-on-1s are a time to discuss long-term objectives and strategy rather than simply day-to-day tasks.

Tim has had the chance to lead many 1-on-1s of his own through the years at multiple companies. His advice is to get to know each team member on a personal level. Take a genuine interest in their lives. Work together with your team members to create shared expectations for their projects and their development, then hold them accountable to those expectations.

There are many ways to conduct effective 1-on-1s. Regardless of how you conduct your 1-on-1s, strive for direct communication, honesty, and vulnerability in these meetings.

1-on-1 Tips

- **Prioritize your 1-on-1s.** These meetings are one of the best ways to connect with team members and determine where the team needs assistance. Treat your 1-on-1s as a priority and avoid canceling them at the last minute.

- **Determine who is running the meeting.** Decide whether you or the team member is setting the agenda for the meetings. Whoever schedules the meeting should set it up as a recurring calendar invite—otherwise, it's too easy to forget about meeting regularly.

- **Keep notes.** Jot down what you and the team member discussed so you can revisit those goals and ideas later. Some managers even track their notes in an ongoing Google Doc that is shared with the employee, so both people can see past discussion points and action items.

Additional Resources

Article:
"How to Make Your One-on-Ones with Employees More Productive"
by Rebecca Knight (*Harvard Business Review*)

Book:
Fierce Conversations
by Susan Scott

Book:
Radical Candor
by Kim Scott

Book:
The Coaching Habit
by Michael Bungay Stanier

TED Talk:
"The Power of Vulnerability"
by Brené Brown

Tool:
Lighthouse (GetLighthouse.com) is a tool that you can use to ask better questions and track information for 1-on-1s

CHAPTER 13
CAREER PATH DEVELOPMENT

"The best leaders help people with more than their jobs...They help them to become better people, not just better workers."
-JOHN MAXWELL

As you know, career advancement looks a lot different at Gravity than it does at other companies. This means that career path conversations with employees also look different here than they do anywhere else. The goal of this chapter is to give you a mental framework and some shared language for talking to team members about how to advance within the company.

Employees Are Not Defined by Roles/Titles
We don't believe that career advancement looks like climbing a ladder. Employees here are not defined by their role or title, but rather by the value they provide to the organization.

When we walk into meetings, we should check our titles at

the door. A person's title should have no bearing on whether others view their ideas as good or bad. What matters is making the right decision for our company and clients—regardless of who suggests the idea. We want a Finance Analyst who started at our company yesterday to have equal ability to impact our decisions as our CEO or CTO.

Management Is Not the Only Path to Advancement

In many companies, the best (or only) way to advance is to get promoted into a management role. This creates an environment where each person is fighting for a role in management even if they don't really want to manage people. Because they want to make more money, and management is the path to more money, they feel they need to climb up the corporate ladder.

We don't want an environment like that. Some people have a passion and proficiency for managing people, whereas others do not. Forcing each person to become a manager in order for them to advance and make more money is equivalent to shoving square pegs in round roles. It's a bad fit for both the employee and the organization. No one benefits.

Instead, we want to create an environment that rewards people who become better at their jobs, continuously add value to the company, and find ways to help our company succeed. That means someone could have a successful career here without ever stepping foot in management.

We want employees to recognize that sometimes advancement here looks like making a lateral move to bring their skills and knowledge into another department. Sometimes it means creating a new role that is a perfect fit for their passion, skills, and the company's needs. And yes, sometimes advancement is moving into a management role. The point is, there are many ways to progress within our company, and some of those ways are not intuitive.

"Creator" vs. "Consumer"

The vast majority of employees around the world exhibit a "consumer" mindset in their jobs. They assume the current reality is the only reality. They treat their company's structure, work culture, and current processes as unchangeable. They evaluate the relative merits of different employment opportunities based on these attributes as they exist at the time, just like a shopper evaluating different pairs of jeans.

We don't want employees here to be consumers. We want employees to be "creators." Help employees challenge the status quo and work toward creating the company they want to work for. Part of building a career here is creating an environment that supports everyone doing their best work.

As far as careers go at Gravity, the people who best embody the "creator" mindset are the ones who go on to do incredible things. They're the people who create new products, departments, and innovative ideas that push us forward. Being a "creator" is the best way to develop a successful career at Gravity.

For example, if one of your team members thinks we should create a new department to handle a specific type of work, encourage them to explore that idea further. Help them consider what questions we'd need to answer as a company before determining whether creating a new team would be the right move.

Risk Leads to Stability

At most companies, taking risks can endanger your career. At some companies, if you create a new product that doesn't meet the needs of the market, you could lose your job. That's not how things work here.

We value progress and innovation, and we know that the only way to improve is by trying new things. Trying new things is inherently risky; it's a departure from the status quo. We realize that when we try new things, there is the potential (and sometimes likelihood) of failure, but we innovate nonetheless.

We believe in a counterintuitive idea: taking calculated risks is the best way to have stability and job security. Individuals who don't try new things and exhibit a passion for progress tend to not succeed at our company.

Career Planning

Remember that the first bullet point on our Employee Bill of Rights is the right to develop compensation goals and a career development plan with your manager. We'll talk about that concept more in the chapter on Compensation, but overall, it's important for us to work with each team member to develop a personal career plan for what they'd like to do within the company. Each person's career plan will probably change many times, but that's no reason not to have a career plan.

Employees who don't develop a career and compensation plan sometimes start to feel like there is little opportunity for advancement at Gravity because there is no predefined path. We don't want employees to make that mistake, so it's important for us to work with them to develop a plan together.

Career Path Tips

Master your current role. Emphasize with employees that their job is to master their current role and continuously learn more about our company while being a strong team player. The best way to achieve your next role is to knock it out of the park in your current one.

De-emphasize titles. When you're helping an employee develop a career plan, focus on what skills they want to use and what challenges they want to solve rather than what role they want to attain. For instance, rather than focusing directly on helping someone become a Deployment Manager, focus on helping them develop their leadership and management skills, solve difficult problems on the team, and handle escalated issues. Those abilities are all needed in the Deployment Manager role, and by working on those things, you're helping them get there by focusing on skill development rather than obtaining a title.

Exercise creative leadership. Sometimes the best path for a team member isn't immediately obvious. Their passion and skills may not align with any current role in the company. That's okay. Consider whether we should create a new role that allows them to do what they do best while helping our company succeed.

Additional Resources

Article:
"Stop Striving for a Specific Job Title"
by Bobby Powers (Medium)

E-Learning:
LDU talk on "Managing a Team"
by Rosita Barlow

Highlights Blog:
Careers at Gravity blog series

CHAPTER 14
PERFORMANCE MANAGEMENT

"I think you should constantly be managing performance."
-TAMMI KROLL

Performance management is helping each employee do their best work. It is a simple, yet difficult process. Effective performance management requires two things:
1. Setting clear expectations for team members
2. Holding team members accountable to those expectations

Setting Clear Expectations
Setting clear expectations for the team is the foundation of performance management. *Do team members know what is expected of them? Do they know what great performance looks like?* If we haven't clarified our expectations, we cannot expect the team to meet our expectations.

Even when you do share your expectations, you need to confirm that each team member heard what you were trying to say. You may think you've clearly communicated a message, but you failed to mention a few critical things. Or perhaps a few of the words or phrases you used meant something different to the other person.

Everyone's mind works differently, so it's important to confirm that you and the employee have a shared understanding of what they need to accomplish in their role.

> "The single biggest problem in communication is the illusion that it has taken place."
> -GEORGE BERNARD SHAW

Setting clear expectations is not a one-time thing. It is an ongoing conversation as the team member's skills improve and our clients' needs evolve. We should constantly reset and redefine expectations to ensure each team member knows what we expect of them.

Holding Team Members Accountable

Beyond setting clear expectations, the next component of performance management is holding each person accountable to those expectations. Many managers struggle with this step because it can sometimes involve difficult conversations. As a manager, it's your responsibility to provide immediate, candid feedback and hold your team accountable for producing great work. If someone continues to struggle to meet expectations, you need to talk to them and share what you've observed.

"I used to think holding people accountable would impact their confidence, but in reality, it's often the opposite," Tammi Kroll says. "Most people want to be held accountable. They want to know what your expectations are and they want to work for someone who has very high expectations."

What Causes Performance Issues?

Every person *wants* to produce great work. There is not a single employee who desires to perform poorly in their job. So why do people sometimes struggle?

Performance issues are generally related to one of two things: motivation or ability. Either the person lacks the motivation to do their job effectively or they lack the ability to perform at a high level. The two problems have different solutions.

Overall, we want to approach performance issues from a perspective of understanding rather than judgment. Jena Miller (Employee Relations) says our focus shouldn't be "You didn't do this" but rather "What went wrong?" Seek to understand the underlying cause of the problem. Asking questions and understanding the *why* behind performance struggles is a much more empathetic response than immediately judging the person for doing a poor job.

> "For every hundred men hacking away at the branches of a diseased tree, only one will stoop to inspect the roots."
> -CHINESE PROVERB

Motivation Problems

Motivation problems are sometimes caused by personal issues outside of work. It's hard to concentrate if your marriage is struggling, your mom just died, or you're struggling with crippling depression.

Whenever possible, we should strive to know our employees well enough to know what's going on in their personal lives so we can help accommodate difficult life situations. Ask yourself questions like the following: *How can I determine what is causing their work struggles? How can I support them as a person rather than just as an employee?*

However, we also want to protect that employee's right to privacy. If the team member doesn't want to share personal details, don't force them to do so. And if you get the hint that the issue could be related to a health or medical problem, advise the employee to partner with our Team Advocates team.

Sometimes an employee's lack of motivation is not connected to any significant life event. It's possible they're simply struggling to overcome fear or exhaustion. The point is that we don't know what is causing a performance issue until we take the time to ask questions and dive in further.

Here are a few ideas for how to overcome motivation problems:

- **Connect back to their motivators.** Jena advises finding out what is important to that team member, then connecting their work and performance back to their intrinsic motivators. For example, perhaps one of your team members has expressed that they really want to move into a management role, yet they refuse to give direct feedback to their coworkers. You could draw the connection back to their career goals to remind them that feedback is critical to successful leadership, and in order to become a manager down the road, they will need to develop that skill.

- **Clarify expectations.** Check in with the team member to ensure they have a clear understanding of your expectations. It's hard for people to be motivated when they don't understand where they're heading and why. Clearly articulate your expectations and talk about anticipated roadblocks that could prevent the employee from meeting expectations. It's much easier for team members to overcome challenges when they're expecting them and already have a game plan for defeating them.

- **Identify demotivators.** Ask the employee if you or others have done anything recently that has been a de-motivator for them. For example, it's possible that you recently micromanaged the employee on a project and made them feel like they had little autonomy to make decisions. Micromanagement is often de-motivating, so it would be helpful to know if that is impacting that employee's current performance. It's important to note that we cannot motivate someone else. Motivation is an internal thing. However, even though we cannot motivate someone to want to do something, we *can* remove de-motivators that stand in their way.

Ability Problems

Ability problems could be the result of poor training, increasing job expectations, mis-hiring, or misalignment of skill set and job role. If the person clearly is motivated to work hard and stay engaged but they're still struggling to meet expectations, you are likely dealing with an ability problem.

Similar to dealing with motivation problems, the first thing to do is to ask questions and collect more information rather than jumping to conclusions. Ask the employee questions like the following: *Do you feel like you received sufficient training to perform this work? What can I do to help? What aspect of this project is most difficult for you?*

Authors David Whetten and Kim Cameron[16] suggest a few ideas for how to overcome ability problems:

- **Resupply** - Ensure the team member has the resources and support they need to do their job effectively.

- **Retrain** - Offer additional training. It's possible that we didn't

---

[16] Whetten, David A., and Kim S. Cameron. *Developing Management Skills*. Prentice Hall, 2010.

set the employee up for success in their role in the first place.

- **Refit** - Consider rearranging the employee's job tasks around their unique strengths. You could reassign some of the person's work to another team member (either for the short-term or long-term) and move more tasks onto the person's plate that align with their skills.

- **Reassign** - It's possible that the employee is a great fit for the company but not a great fit for their current role. If you think that's the case, start talking to other team leaders to see if it would make sense to transfer the person into a different team.

- **Release** - Sometimes the best solution is to let the person go. This is our last resort, but it's occasionally the best option for everyone involved. We need an environment where everyone performs at a high level, and the employee wants to work somewhere where they feel successful. If that's the case, partner with Team Advocates to determine an offboarding plan for the employee.

How to Create a Performance Improvement Plan

If an employee is struggling, you should work together with the employee to create a plan for improvement. A performance improvement plan (PIP) is an agreed-upon plan that contains next steps and SMART (specific, measurable, attainable, relevant, and time-bound) goals for what the employee should complete and by when.

When writing a PIP, we must explicitly state the performance gap we've observed and explain what must be done to fix it. As much as possible, it's important for the employee to own the plan so they can be in charge of their own growth and development.

A PIP is distinguished from a standard performance conversation in a few key ways:

- It is a formal document that you'll send to the employee.
- It explicitly conveys the seriousness of the performance issues.
- It contains defined steps for improvement in written format.
- It goes into their employee file.

If one of your team members continues to struggle despite repeated conversations about their performance, reach out to Employee Relations and Team Advocates. You can work with them to decide if a PIP could help in this situation.

Performance Management Tips

⊛ **Don't wait until there is a problem.** You should have ongoing performance discussions with your team. Don't let something develop into a big problem before you bring it up. Talk about any concerns as you have them.

⊛ **Dig deep to understand the why.** Every performance issue happens for a reason. You want to understand that reason in order to deal with it appropriately.

⊛ **Be candid, kind, and assertive.** Similar to what we discussed in the "Giving Feedback" chapter, it's important to balance candor and kindness when sharing tough messages. Don't sugarcoat the message. If an employee is struggling, tell them. Share what you've observed.

⊛ **Care for your team members as people.** Find ways to support the "whole person" by learning more about each person's life, family, hobbies, and passions. Caring for someone does *not* mean you would never fire them. It means that you will first do everything possible to help them succeed.

Learn each employee's strengths and weaknesses.
It's okay to have weaknesses. Everyone has them. The important thing is to understand them so we can develop those weaknesses and/or work around them. Knowing someone's strengths and weaknesses will also help you move them into the best role for their abilities.

Delegate work to develop and determine ability.
"Sometimes you delegate to a weakness; sometimes you delegate to a strength," Jena says. "If you're not delegating, you're not giving yourself an opportunity to assess performance."

Trust, but verify. If someone is struggling with a task, check their work occasionally to verify that it's being completed to the standard you expect.

Eliminate subjectivity. If you conduct quarterly or annual formal performance reviews with your team, create a rubric with defined criteria for each score. If you include a 1-5 performance scoring system or something similar, define exactly what constitutes a "4" as opposed to a "5." If possible, provide some type of tangible example for each score. The more clear you can be, the more you will eliminate the subjectivity and implicit bias that negatively affect performance reviews.[17]

Give people a chance to improve. Unless an employee committed an egregious offense that warrants immediate termination, we want to work together with them to create a performance improvement plan to help them become more productive and successful.

---

[17] Mackenzie, Lori, JoAnne Wehner, and Shelley Correll. "Why Most Performance Evaluations Are Biased, and How to Fix Them." *HBR*, 2019.

Don't tolerate mediocrity. We want a stellar team. If someone is underperforming and we allow them to continue underperforming, everyone suffers. Some members of the team will become frustrated and may even decide to leave the company. Other team members may think they can slack off because we seem to allow that behavior. We *must* hold a high bar for success.

 # Additional Resources

Article:
"Dealing With Poor Performance: Lack of Ability, or Low Motivation?"
by the Mind Tools Content Team

Article:
"How to Hold Your Team Accountable"
by Dave Bailey (Medium)

Book:
How to Win Friends and Influence People
by Dale Carnegie

Book:
The One Minute Manager
by Ken Blanchard and Spencer Johnson

Partner with Team Advocates (TA)

CHAPTER 15
INTERVIEWING AND HIRING

"Hiring people is an art, not a science, and resumes can't tell you whether someone will fit into a company's culture."
-HOWARD SCHULTZ

One of the most important things you'll ever do as a leader is hire great people. Hiring the right team member will positively impact not only team productivity, but the job satisfaction of other employees, the happiness of our merchants and partners, and our long-term profitability.

On the flipside, a mis-hire conservatively costs one-third of that person's annual salary. After accounting for indirect costs like training time, lost customers, and team disruption, some estimates even say that mis-hires could cost six figures.[18] In that

[18] Fatemi, Falon. "The True Cost of a Bad Hire—It's More Than You Think." Forbes, 2016.

way, hiring is an activity that amplifies good or bad decisions; the ripple effects last for years.

What Are We Looking For?

Many of the traits we're looking for apply to any role within the company. In addition to finding people who will share our three core values of Creative Leadership, Passion for Progress, and Responsibility, we want to find people who are comfortable working autonomously and who love to solve problems. People who succeed at Gravity are often insatiably curious, lifelong learners who are open to feedback and always looking to improve.

Jose Garcia, who has served as Deployment Supervisor and Lead Culture Consultant, looks for three specific traits in anyone he hires:

1. **Humble** - They put the team, our merchants, and our partners ahead of themselves
2. **Hungry** - They relentlessly dig to solve problems and learn new things
3. **Smart** - They are able to think creatively, exercise good judgment, and act with emotional intelligence

Jose adds that each role demands additional specific traits. As the manager, you need to know your team and what they will need from the new hire in order to be successful. This could be technical job knowledge or it could be a particular trait like optimism, candor, or kindness.

> "There's only one interview technique that matters... Do your homework so you can listen to the answers and react to them and ask follow-ups. Do your homework, prepare."
> -JIM LEHRER

Before bringing people in for interviews, decide exactly what you're looking for in a new hire. Work with the recruiter to develop a list of "needs" and "wants" for candidates. This will help you create your basic hiring rubric for the position. For instance, if you're hiring a Deployment Rep, you may decide the person *needs* to have some past technical experience with equipment, computers, or networks and you may *want* them to also have past customer service experience. In other words, it's not a deal-breaker if a candidate has never worked in a service role before, but it would be if they had never worked in a technical role.

You'll then evaluate all of the candidates against this rubric to see how they stack up against each other. Brainstorm creative questions that will help you see whether the candidate exhibits the desired traits or has the relevant experience for the job. For instance, notice the difference between these questions:

- "Do you think you could flourish in a fast-moving, autonomous environment?" → *"What is your ideal work environment?"* or *"Describe your ideal workday."*

- "How do you typically function under stress?" → *"Give me an example of a stressful situation you've faced recently."*

- "Do you see yourself working here?" → *"From what you've seen so far, what do you like and dislike about our work culture?"*

The questions on the left are limiting, more closed-ended, and imply a right answer and a wrong answer. The questions on the right allow us to hear a more complete, honest answer from the candidate, which gives us more information to decide whether they're the right fit.

Regardless of how good your questions may be, you will inevitably need to dig deeper and ask detailed follow-up questions. "Not everybody will give you a great answer to a great interview question," says Marta Anthony (Recruiter). "It's more about going deeper and asking follow-up questions to candidates. Listen to what is said and what is not said."

Unconscious Bias

It's easy to form snap judgments of candidates from what we see or hear on paper, on the phone, or in person. We may think their resume is poorly formatted, their work experience is inadequate, or their college grades were abysmal. We may meet them and form a snap judgment that they are too self-assured, too shy, or too different from us. We all have biases of some sort. Many of these biases are not conscious choices, yet they impact our actions in subtle, dangerous ways.

"Everyone's going to have bias going into an interview. Studies show that people make most decisions within eight seconds or less," says Alex Franklin (Sales Recruiter). "In the context of an interview, that can be pretty scary because you generally have an hour booked, and you're probably making some kind of judgment in your first eight seconds."

Alex's advice: "You almost have to acknowledge the bias in order to move past it." Be open to surprises. It's a problem if you never change your mind after forming an initial impression of someone. Alex has hired many individuals who have gone on to do incredible things at Gravity, including Phil Akhavan. Alex shares that when he first looked at Phil's interview packet (resume, application, cover letter, etc.), he was not impressed with Phil's prior work experience or the way he presented the information. Alex thought the interview would be short and he'd move on to the next candidate. Alex's first impression was wrong. Phil ended up being a stellar candidate who went on to manage our Inside Sales team, and Alex is elated that he hired Phil.

Jose Garcia and Marta Anthony offer similar advice about overcoming unconscious bias in interviews. They both use the tactic of trying to disprove their initial impression of someone. "The moment I feel that I really like or dislike someone, I spend the rest of the interview trying to disprove that," says Jose. Jose asks himself, "How am I going to make sure I'm fair to this person?"

Marta believes that a lot of the process of eliminating unconscious bias happens even before the job role is posted. We can be fair to each candidate by creating an objective definition of what we need and want in a candidate. The better our hiring rubric for the role, the less we need to rely on intuition and snap judgments. "We cannot just say, 'This person isn't a good fit for the team,'" Marta says. "It's natural to want to hire someone you will like, but that's not what we're doing here. We're building a great company, and how much you like someone is not enough and should never be at the front of the decision-making process."

When we make hiring decisions based upon gut instinct and how much we like someone, we often make poor decisions. "When I've made mis-hires, they've been people I see myself in and I don't remain objective," Jose says. This is one of the reasons why candidates always interview with multiple people. We want to get a well-rounded perspective of each candidate, and including multiple decision-makers in the process helps with that.

Interviewing Tips

 Avoid groupthink. After each interview round, ensure every interviewer has a chance to share their feedback without their impression getting biased by other interviewers. You can minimize groupthink in a few ways. One way is to ask the least junior interviewer for their opinion first so they aren't influenced by the senior interviewers. Another way is to have interviewers individually fill out a scorecard before they debrief with the other interviewers.

- **Build a hiring scorecard or rubric.** Know what you're looking for. Know what is non-negotiable versus what is a "wish list" item.

- **Weight which characteristics you need.** Assign a weight to each desired trait for this role based on its relative importance in what you want from this new hire. For instance, here's a basic weight scale that Jose used for filling a recent Tech Support position:
  - 40% - Technical knowledge
  - 25% - Professionalism on the phone
  - 25% - Relationship with the team
  - 10% - Past job experience

- **Think about "culture add" instead of "culture fit."** Companies often talk about whether someone is a good "culture fit." That mentality can lead to serious bias and lack of diversity because people end up hiring others who look and sound like them. We don't want that mentality here. Don't just hire "yourself" (i.e., someone with a similar DISC profile, personality type, past experience). We want diverse teams full of people with unique, creative ideas. Think in terms of whether or not the person will add to our culture and make it better.

- **Prepare before every interview.** Before you speak with someone, our company and the applicant have taken the time to fill out multiple documents: TTI assessment, phone screen notes, resume, job application, career history form, etc. Spend the time to review the interview packet before the interview. Alex Franklin says when he first became a hiring manager, he would spend 30-60 minutes preparing for each interview. Now that he's given hundreds of interviews, his prep time has moved down to 15-30 minutes. Prioritize the time to prepare for each interview. It's important, so make the time for it.

Avoid business jargon. Many people use business buzzwords because they think doing so will make them sound intelligent or sophisticated. However, most buzzwords don't convey much real information. As the interviewer, you should avoid jargon and encourage the candidate to avoid it as well. Rather than talking about "streamlining" and offering "innovative people solutions," make the candidate tell you specifically how they made processes more efficient and solved people issues in their past company.

Dig deeper. The best insights of any interview often come from follow-up questions rather than initial questions. Take the time to pry further into the candidate's answers to understand their full perspective and learn more about how they make decisions.

Avoid gut decisions. Identify two or three things you want to answer during each interview to determine whether to move the candidate on to the next stage of the process. Find a way to see them in a job-related setting. It's often useful to see the candidate perform some type of job-related task. Consider including a role play, homework assignment, or job-related exercise as part of the interview process.

Debrief and self-assess after each interview. Take the time to give and get feedback from the other interviewers after the interview process. Doing a quick retrospective will give you insights on where you need to prepare more, ask better-worded questions, or dive deeper to learn more about candidates.

Sleep on it. Sometimes it's best to consider your decision overnight. If you're not excited about the person the next day, that could be a sign that they're not the right fit.

- **Hire on skills and characteristics rather than work experience.** Many of our best Sales Reps have not come in with sales experience. Similarly, many of our best Support Reps have not explicitly worked in customer service roles previously. Look for capability and skill set rather than items on a resume. We hire people, not resumes.

- **Be patient.** Know that the cost of a mis-hire is really high. It's better to spend more time to find the right person than to rush into a decision because you really want to fill a role.

Additional Resources

Article:
"What Is the True Cost of Hiring a Bad Employee?"
by Jörgen Sundberg (Undercover Recruiter blog)

Book:
Work Rules!
by Laszlo Bock

Book:
The Ideal Team Player
by Patrick Lencioni

E-Learning:
All-employee training "DISC: What Is It Good For?"
by Ian Nisbet

CHAPTER 16
COMPENSATION

"The purpose of an organization is to make the humans'
lives better."

-DAN PRICE

Money is viewed as one of the biggest taboo topics in our
society. It seems like people are more comfortable discussing
politics, religion, and their personal lives before they talk about
how much they earn, how much they spend, and what types of
financial goals they have. As a result, it can often feel awkward
having a conversation with team members about their financial
goals, and they might not be immediately forthcoming with
their thoughts or questions.

At Gravity, we want employees to be comfortable asking
the hard questions—and that includes questions about
compensation. Rather than treating compensation like a

black box topic as many other companies do, we want to frequently engage in conversations about compensation and encourage team members to share their thoughts. That's why we talk about compensation in the very first bullet point on our Employee Bill of Rights: Develop a specific annual compensation goal with your manager.

Compensation Conversation Frequency

Make compensation conversations a priority. Rather than shying away from the discussion, engage openly with each team member to learn more about their desired compensation trajectory. The more frequently you have these conversations, the less opportunity there is for you to lose track of your team member's goals and targets. As an added benefit, over time, each of you will become more comfortable having these conversations.

We recommend having a compensation conversation with each team member at least once every three months. If your team member has not already reached out to you about having one of these conversations, reach out to them and say you'd like to discuss their compensation goals and personal business plan.

We want to make money less of a distraction, not more of one. When employees are secure in their financial position and clear about where they are going, they can focus on what matters most—serving our clients. These conversations also encourage employees to consider opportunities within the company before seeking financial gain or promotion outside the company.

The goal of each compensation conversation is twofold:
- Discuss the employee's personal financial plan. Get clarity from the employee on their financial goals for the near future (i.e., What salary do they want to be earning in the next 2, 5, or 10+ years?).
- Jointly create a personal business plan. Work together

to create a career progression plan that will allow the employee to attain their desired salary level.

Creating a Personal Financial Plan

Start by asking the employee about their long-term financial goals. However they choose to define "long-term" is fine, but try to get them to think as far in the future as they can. Doing so will allow them to develop a grander vision and more runway to achieve aggressive financial goals.

Some people will have an entire financial plan mapped out to the penny while others will not have thought about financial goals whatsoever. If the employee has identified specific financial goals, you can move straight into talking about their business plan and career progression plan.

If they need more help, ask about any major life goals that will require significant financial resources. Do they want to buy a house? Put a kid through college? Get out of debt? Retire to France by age 45?

Once they have articulated these goals, challenge them to think about what they will need to make these things happen. You may need to give the employee some time to think about this part. If that's the case, be sure to set a deadline so you can continue the conversation.

Creating a Personal Business Plan

Once the employee has established a personal financial plan, you can work together to develop a business plan that will allow them to achieve their compensation goals. The idea is to come up with specific goals that, if met, will align with their personal financial plan.

At Gravity, we want everyone to be in a position where they are contributing more to the company than they are taking. This encourages risk-taking and a bias for action, rather than a feeling of fear and of being trapped. The marriage between the business plan and the personal financial plan should take this into account.

Depending on how aggressive the employee's financial plan is, you may need to push the team member hard on their goals and be brutally honest about the day-to-day effort required to achieve those goals. If you believe the financial goals are unrealistic and can't find a business plan that will match these goals, you may have to go back and re-evaluate the financial goals together. (For more information on setting compensation levels, see the questions at the end of this chapter.)

Here are a few example goals employees can work toward in their personal business plans to add more value to the company:

- Completing a major project
- Switching roles within the company to bring their strengths and insight to a different position or team
- Taking on additional responsibility (e.g. becoming the CEO of a project designed to reduce client attrition, taking ownership of a specific partnership)
- Increasing output/efficiency (which could be measured by the number of cases closed, dollars in revenue generated, dollars in costs saved, etc.)

Keep in mind, however, that the priorities of the company, department, and individual employee might change over time, and we don't want the employee to feel like their compensation is tied to achieving a specific goal at all costs. We don't want people focused so much on a given metric that they lose sight of other important aspects of their role.

Instead, these personal business plan goals should be used as guidelines and benchmarks by which you and the employee can track progress over time, checking in regularly to see if the specific priorities have changed. It's possible that the two of you are able to come up with a way to bring even more value to the company than described in the original plan. If that's the case, don't be afraid to pivot and pursue that new, improved path.

Once the plan is in place, agree to evaluate it with the employee at regular intervals and make it clear that the plan is not set in stone. Set a date for when you will check in next so the employee keeps the conversation in mind as they progress. The plan will change over time, but you should both work together on those changes, so you are both on the same page.

Questions to Ask to Help Determine Compensation

- What impact is this person having on our company mission?
- Would you enthusiastically rehire this person if they applied today?
- What compensation would you offer to their replacement?
- How do they value present compensation vs. future compensation?
- What is the market value for the job this person is doing?
- How much is pay distracting them from their work?
- Do they have a history of hitting their goals?
- Do they have a history of high performance?
- How are they performing compared to their peers?
- How are they being paid compared to their peers?
- Are they in a place where they are giving more than they are taking?

In general, we want to engage in these complex conversations rather than shying away from them. We won't always have the right answers, and that's okay. There's no set formula for determining the appropriate compensation for a team member; each situation is different.

The important thing is to exhibit the courage to conduct these compensation conversations. Ensure that you and the team members are on the same page. Once you have shared expectations, you can jointly work on a plan for how to meet those expectations.

Compensation Tips

Ask questions. If an employee asks for a large increase or says they need more money in order to do XYZ in their personal life, try to understand where they're coming from. Ask about what factors are driving their request and how will they achieve the value.

Understand the employee's benchmarks. If an employee implies that they think they're underpaid, ask questions to understand what benchmark they're using to reach that conclusion (e.g., a website, survey data). If you want, you can partner with Team Advocates to perform a thorough compensation analysis.

You don't need to respond immediately. If a team member raises a difficult compensation question, it's perfectly fine for you to ask for some time to think about it. Tell them you need time for consideration, then follow-up with them in a timely manner.

Set appropriate expectations. We should educate our teams that a quarterly wage increase should not always be expected but that a quarterly compensation review conversation is encouraged. Compensation increases when it is deserved.

Our goal is to increase every person's salary. Even if someone is doing a job that the broader job market deems to be worth less than our living wage, we still want to find a way to gradually and continually increase that person's salary over time. Although we don't want to set the expectation that team members will receive compensation increases every quarter, as employees continue to grow and improve, they deserve more pay.

When you give a salary increase, explain why. Tie compensation increases back to why that employee is receiving the increase. Increases are more impactful when you can tie them back to why.

Think about long-term sustainability. If you give an employee a big compensation increase, they may be disappointed if their next increase isn't as large. Consider the long-term impact of any compensation decisions you make. If the employee completes a large goal or milestone, reward them with a commensurate compensation increase but explain that they're receiving a larger increase than normal because they accomplished a larger milestone.

Compensation isn't tied to a title. "It's okay to have someone on your team who is paid more than you as a manager," Tammi says. "We all have different roles in this company, and we have different responsibilities within that role. One person's role isn't more important than another's role."

Consider a small bump for encouragement. Tammi says, "Counterintuitively, if you have someone who hasn't been performing well but you know they're able to perform, sometimes giving them a small compensation bump can be a way to show that you believe in them and you're investing in them and this is what you need to see from them."

Reaffirm the employee's importance. If an employee asks for a really small increase, it could be a signal that they lack self-confidence or don't realize how much value they add to the company. Take the time to recognize the team member's achievements and let them know how much you appreciate their work. Consider surprising them with a higher increase than they've requested.

 # Additional Resources

Article:
"The Imaginary Value of Money"
by Dan Price (Medium)

Article:
"What Is an Employee Worth?"
by Dan Price (Medium)

Book:
Drive
by Dan Pink

Video:
"The Surprising Truth About What Motivates Us"
by RSA Animate

CONCLUSION

"What you leave behind is not what is engraved in stone monuments, but what is woven into the lives of others."

-PERICLES

Learning how to become a better leader and manager is a lifelong quest. We hope the concepts you've read in this book will help you as you begin that quest, but what you do from here is up to you. This book started the discussion, but it's up to you to continue it.

Use the stories and ideas from this book to spark conversations with other Gravity leaders. Find a mentor who can challenge you to lead with the right mixture of confidence and humility. Seek out feedback from your team members, peers, and manager. Select two or three of the books, articles, TED talks, and LDU trainings mentioned in this book as your next resources on your leadership journey.

As a leader, you have an opportunity to improve the lives of many. Your leadership legacy will be the people whom you have empowered, encouraged, supported, and developed to become not only better employees, but also better friends, partners, sons, daughters, fathers, mothers, and citizens. Being a leader is an incredible responsibility and gift.

What will you do with that gift?

APPENDICES

MANAGER EXPECTATIONS

As a manager or supervisor, you are responsible for the development of your team as well as the development of your individual team members.

The expectations below are not meant to be an exhaustive list of your duties, but rather a basis for guidance.

- Communicate and develop specific annual career and compensation goals with each team member

- Work with each team member to develop a clear plan to meet their specific career and compensation goals

- Set 2-3 quarterly SMART (Specific, Measurable, Attainable, Relevant, Time-Bound) goals with each team member

- Hold regular one-on-one meetings with each team member to provide feedback, receive feedback, discuss personal development, and set goals for improvement

- Hold quarterly performance and compensation reviews with each team member

- Hold regular department meetings (at least once per quarter)

- Utilize department entertainment budget at least once per quarter

- Push your team to develop relationships with our clients to better understand their needs and ensure their satisfaction

- Always question and challenge the status quo

- Empower your team members to make wise, well-thought, win-win decisions

- Be tactful and strategic when you communicate with our merchants, your team members, other employees, and your manager

- Provide recommendations to your manager when decisions need to be made

- Ensure that your department is providing the best possible service to our customers

- Set the example for conduct and professionalism at all times

- Foster growth and development among your team members

- Live the Gravity Values: Creative Leadership, Passion for Progress, and Responsibility

- Be a leader, make the hard decisions

Manager Development Goals

Additionally, it's helpful to set your own goals for what you want to focus on as a manager. Here are a couple of examples of what this could look like:

- I will ask for four pieces of feedback from my team to understand how I'm doing as a manager.

- I will seek out two people to mentor me, one inside Gravity and one from somewhere else.

What are your manager development goals?

_____

_____

_____

_____

EMPLOYEE EXPECTATIONS

*Note: This document is provided to all employees when they start at Gravity.

Ultimate goal: To think and act like a business owner

Expectations as an employee to be successful at work
1. Cultural expectations
2. Expectations of your work

Cultural expectations
1. We always seek to move forward
    a. Ask questions that would move forward and not create barriers
        i. Forward change is progress
    b. Proactively give us fresh perspective
        i. Many of us are used to the processes we have in

place and may not notice areas for improvement
- c. Amend mistakes even if they are not necessarily your own
2. Understand why
   - a. Learn by observing and asking a lot of progressive questions
   - b. Question things you don't understand
     - i. Never just do things because you were told to
3. Communication
   - a. Be careful of how you communicate to people
     - i. You represent the company
     - ii. Recognize who your customers are and treat them like customers
       1. Your customers can be both internal (operations and sales employees) and external (merchants)
       2. Treat them with the best possible customer service
       3. Don't battle, be partners to help each other out
   - b. Recognize implications of what you're communicating (via email or verbal)
     - i. How is this going to affect the company?
     - ii. How will my communication be received?
     - iii. What are potential problems that can come out of it?
   - c. When sending out mass emails blind copy to make sure people are communicating with you and not to the mass
     - i. Have multiple eyes check over email
     - ii. Even if you have others look over your message, you are ultimately the person responsible for sending it out, so make sure that you're confident in it as well
   - d. Address problems and concerns with person at hand before going to anyone else
     - i. Seek productivity from frustrating conversations
     - ii. Or seek advice from your manager, but he/she will not be the middleman

4. Debates & Disagreement
    a.   Healthy disagreement and debate is important to our overall success and innovation. Therefore, we need to search for and encourage disagreement and open debate.
    b.   Know that not everyone is comfortable speaking up, so we need to work hard to create space for everyone to have their voice heard.
    c.   Be open-minded. We should only care about the best decision, not whose idea it was.
    d.   In rare situations where a mutual decision can't be reached after discussion, bring in another person (e.g., leadership) to hear all points and make the final decision
5. Confidentiality
    a.   There is not any information that you own or have the rights to, so be careful who you disclose to
        i.   Seek to understand before giving confidential information
            1.   "Why do you need that information?"
            2.   "I don't know, let me look into it and get back to you."
        ii.   Keep private information private
            1.   Use secure print to not leave things lying on the printers
            2.   Lock computer
        iii. Discuss confidential information in private space
        iv. Don't discuss confidential information you've overheard
    b.   Use discretion and tact
        i.   Don't answer unasked questions when dealing with confidential information
        ii. Communicate in a way that is productive
        iii. Act with honesty and integrity, but also be very tactful
            1.   Stay objective in what needs to be communicated, and what doesn't/shouldn't be communicated
            2.   Do a minor cost-benefit analysis: if there

are there more cons than pros, then seek alternatives
3. Is there a better mode of communication?

Expectations of your work
1. You are accountable for your time, projects, tasks, and learning
    a. If there are no deadlines, set them yourself
    b. If you can't meet a deadline, communicate (ask for extension or notify of delay) or delegate
    c. You are ultimately responsible for the projects and tasks getting accomplished and accomplished well
        i. Follow through and follow up
        ii. If you delegate, make sure to follow-up that it's been done with quality
        iii. Act as a team
            1. If the project fails, the team fails
            2. Don't pass blame around
    d. Treat the smaller tasks with as much care and planning as the larger tasks
2. Communication is two-way
    a. At any time, let your manager/team know when you feel you are falling behind
    b. Proactively reach out for any of your needs if they are not currently being met (anything from additional support to compensation)

EMPLOYEE BILL OF RIGHTS

As an employee of Gravity Payments, you have the right to:

- Develop a specific annual compensation goal with your manager
- Develop a specific annual career plan with your manager
- Develop quarterly SMART (Specific, Measurable, Attainable, Relevant, Time-Bound) goals with your manager
- Have regular one-on-one meetings with your manager to receive feedback, and to check in on your quarterly and career goals
- Have quarterly performance reviews with your manager
- Have quarterly compensation reviews with your manager
- Be treated with respect and dignity by all employees
- Develop yourself both personally and professionally

- Open two-way communication between you and your manager
- Exercise your creativity and innovation by improving inefficiencies
- The opportunity to suggest amendments to this Bill of Rights
- Wear flannel on Fridays

*Note: This document is also available in Namely.

Our lawyer says we need this: *The contents of this Bill of Rights are presented as a matter of information only. It is not a condition or term of employment. The provisions of this Bill of Rights are not intended to create nor shall they be construed to constitute contractual obligations or a contract of employment between Gravity Payments and any one or all of its employees. Employment with Gravity Payments is "at-will." This means that the length of your employment is not for any fixed term, unless agreed to in writing, and may be terminated by you or Gravity Payments at any time, for any reason or for no reason, with or without cause, and without prior notice.*

APPENDIX D
MANAGER FAQS

It's important to remember that there are a lot of small, yet important managerial tasks that fall on our shoulders as managers. Employees depend upon us for getting the correct pay on their paychecks, getting time-off approved and scheduled, and a host of other things.

Here are some of the most common questions that arise.

Time Off Requests
Q) *What do I do if one of my employees is sick?*
- Encourage them to go home. They need to get well and avoid getting others sick.
- Make sure their urgent and necessary work for the day is covered.
- When they return, ask them to put in their sick day in Namely.

Q) Where can I go to approve employee time-off requests?
- You'll get an email, and you can just click the link in the email to approve.
- If you have the Namely app, you can also approve time-off requests from there.
- You can also log into Namely and click into "Manage Time Off" under "Admin Tools" on your home page. This shows all of your team's time off requests on one page.

Q) What should I do if an employee wants time off in their first 90 days?
- Employees in their first 90 days may choose to take unpaid time off.
- At your discretion, you may choose to advance them accrued paid time off (PTO).
- If you need assistance with making that judgment, Team Advocates (TA) is available to help.
- Please note: "Accrued PTO" in Namely means the time off will be paid, even if the request is more than what is available. Payroll interprets your approval as this entire request should all be paid. If any portion of their time off is to be unpaid, employees need to separately enter it in "Unpaid Time Off" in Namely.

Q) What happens if an employee wants or needs more than 10 days of PTO in their first year?
- Being present in their first year is essential for their long-term success at Gravity because there's so much to learn.
- However, at your discretion, you may choose to grant them more than the allocated amount of PTO.
- Granting more than the allocated amount of PTO is fairly uncommon, but it is an option.

Employee Health (ADA, FMLA, etc.)
Q) What is FMLA? What do I need to know about it?
- The Family Medical Leave Act (FMLA) is a federal labor law that says companies must offer unpaid and protected time

off when an employee suffers from a qualifying serious health condition or needs to take time off due to a family member's medical condition.

- Employees who have been with the company for at least one year are entitled to FMLA leave periods up to 12 weeks.
- Notify Team Advocates any time someone requests any sort of leave, needs to care for a dependent, or needs time off for a medical procedure.
- Someone from TA will work directly with you or with the employee to navigate any next steps. While the federal law pertains to unpaid time off, our Open PTO policy can run concurrently with FMLA.
- Please see the employee handbook for additional details.

Q) *What is ADA? What do I need to know about it?*
- The Americans with Disabilities Act (ADA) prohibits discrimination against any employees with disabilities. It guarantees fair treatment and equal opportunity to all employees suffering from any type of "disability," as defined by law.
- Sometimes an employee may request an accommodation or we may want to provide an accommodation based on the needs of an employee. For example, when an employee has surgery and can only work at a limited capacity for a period of time, we may offer an accommodation. Another example is that employees with conditions like PTSD or an autism-spectrum disorder may require accommodations in regard to their work environment.
- This can be a tricky area, so please reach out to TA whenever you have a question or concern about one of your employees.

Q) *What employee health information is protected?*
- All personal health information is protected (yours and your employees). Examples of protected information include leave requests, accommodations, pregnancy, and mental health issues—to name a few.

- Any health information you hear about employees should be kept in confidence and communicated only to a member of TA, who can provide guidance on disclosure.

Harassment and Discrimination
Note: We do not tolerate harassment or discrimination of any kind, and it should be immediately reported to TA. See Appendix E for more information on this topic.

Other Common Questions
Q) What should I do if I find out that two of my team members are dating?
- Contact Team Advocates.
- TA will reach out and review the dating contract with both employees.

Q) What do I need to submit when I increase an employee's pay?
- Pay raises need to be put in Namely at least a week before the paycheck on which you want the raise to go into effect.

Q) How do I put in a raise?
- Raises can be submitted in Namely or emailed to payroll@ gravitypayments.com.
- Gravity has 24 payroll periods, so you would need to divide the new salary by 24 and enter that as per pay period total.
- The effective date is when the new "rate" begins. So, if you want the raise to be on the 15th paycheck, the effective date would be the 1st. If you want it on the last paycheck of the month, the effective date would be the 16th.

Q) How do I get someone a company credit card?
- Ask Accounting.

HARASSMENT AND LEGAL CLAIMS

We want to avoid even the appearance of impropriety in dealings with our employees. Strive to understand things from the employee's perspective. Ask yourself: How are we treating this employee versus other employees in similar situations?

We all have implicit biases. Your goal should be to become aware of your own biases and work to overcome them. Do not ignore implicit bias when you see others exhibit it. Talk to them about it.

If You See Something, Say Something

- Address incivility or disrespect on the spot: "This is not something we tolerate," "That sounds disrespectful," etc.
- If you overhear any comment that is even slightly related to harassment or that makes you feel uncomfortable, discuss it with TA immediately.

- You are the model of proper behavior at the company.
- Don't forget third-party harassment (e.g., vendors, merchants, partners).

What You Need to Know

Employees sometimes contact lawyers because they believe they were treated unjustly due to being in a protected class or having a recent disability. The best way to avoid legal concerns is to treat everyone with respect, compassion, and understanding. Partner with TA immediately if anyone mentions or implies any of the following things:

- **Disability (or Accommodation)** - Almost any medical, physical, or mental condition, even a short-term condition (e.g., broken leg), meets the legal definition of a "disability" under federal and state laws. Employers are responsible for providing "reasonable" accommodation for employees with disabilities.
- **Discrimination** - Treating an employee or group of employees differently than another, especially with regard to protected classes (defined on the next page)
- **Harassment** - We will not tolerate any employee disrespecting or demeaning any other employee.
- **Hostile work environment** - We must ensure that our environment provides an opportunity for every employee to do their work without having to worry about discrimination or abuse of any kind. In legal terms, a hostile work environment refers to severe and sustained behavior, actions, or communication over a period of time.
- **Protected activity** - Employees are legally entitled to voice disagreement, join labor unions, ask coworkers about salary information, and report discriminatory behavior, among other things. Companies are not allowed to retaliate against these actions.
- **Quid pro quo** - Refers to an employee or manager promising to do "this for that," especially with regard to sexual favors or other illicit actions
- **Retaliation** - We cannot retaliate or perform "adverse

activity" because an employee has engaged in protected activity.

- **Sexual harassment** - We will not tolerate any employees engaging in unwelcome or inappropriate sexual behavior such as crude jokes or comments, objectifying remarks, or other undesired sexual interactions.

Protected Classes

- Race
- Age
- Political Affiliation
- Religion
- Disability
- Pregnancy
- National Origin
- Marital Status
- Sexual Orientation
- Gender Identity
- Veteran Status
- Engaging in Protected Activity

Overall takeaway: when in doubt, talk to Team Advocates!

Made in the USA
Middletown, DE
03 July 2019